The Supervisor's Problem Solver

W. H. Weiss

amacom

AMERICAN MANAGEMENT ASSOCIATION

This book is available at a special discount when ordered in bulk quantities. For information, contact Special Sales Department, AMACOM, a division of American Management Association, 135 West 50th Street, New York, NY 10020.

Library of Congress Cataloging in Publication Data

Weiss, W. H., 1918-
The supervisor's problem solver.

Includes index.
1. Supervision of employees. I. Title.
HF5549.W43127   1982   658.3'02   82-71324
ISBN 0-8144-5754-1
ISBN 0-81844-7655-4

First AMACOM paperback edition 1986.

Printing Number

10 9 8 7 6 5 4 3 2 1

Preface

In this book I've tried to provide the guidance you need to solve supervisory problems, but my answers certainly are not the absolute ones—life isn't that simple. People and circumstances differ from one problem to another. You will have to judge each problem you face on the job separately, and decide which course of action is best for the employee and the company.

You'll find that many of the problems I've recounted are solved satisfactorily by talking to or counseling employees. But you must be careful when you do this. Avoid getting involved in an employee's emotional problems—leave such matters to psychiatrists and psychologists, who have the proper training. It is very easy for your own feelings and responses to complicate the problem. Empathizing—rather than sympathizing—with a person who has a serious problem will enable you to come to grips with the situation.

W. H. Weiss

Contents

1

The Employee
Who Has a Poor Attitude

Employees who have poor attitudes are a never-ending source of irritation and frustration to supervisors. They exhibit their poor attitude in many different ways, including complaining chronically, avoiding work, and doing an inadequate job, all of which make for poor productivity and unrest. Supervisors should be constantly alert for opportunities to promote and foster good attitudes in people. They need to take immediate action when a worker's poor attitude affects the safety, output, or welfare of that individual or of other employees.

The employee who has a poor attitude toward how much work he does

The Problem

Dick S., a cutter on the beef processing line, was not pleased when the cutters' workloads were increased. The production manager you work for at the meat packing company in Michigan had noticed a work-flow problem on the production line: members of the cutting crew were idle part of the time because carcasses moved rather slowly through their department, while in the processing department (the next step), finishers had too much to do. Company management had decided that the way to correct the imbalance and smooth out the work flow was to give the cutters some of the finishing work.

Dick approached you, his supervisor, during the coffee break on the first day the new work pattern was put in effect. He complained about the extra work he was now expected to do and said that the company should have hired another person in the finishing department rather than transfer part of that department's work to the cutters. You expected Dick to complain; just a few weeks ago he had asked that the conveyer be slowed down because "the work is too hard." He also does a minimal job of washing down at the break periods and tries to pass off this work to other members of the crew when he can. How should you handle Dick? What should you say to him?

The Solution

Explain to Dick that management studied the conditions carefully and fully before deciding to give the cutters some of the finishing work. Because of space limitations, it wouldn't have been practical to add someone to the finishing department. Furthermore, the company was not in a position to hire more people. Operating costs had increased, competition was stiffer, and the company was barely making a profit. (Tell Dick these things, of course, only if they are true.)

Dick may not like your explanation and may continue to complain. If he does, point out that the cutters were actually idle part of the time, and that the additional work they are now being asked to do should not create a hardship for them. Encourage Dick to suggest a better way to handle finishing jobs so that the men would be more efficient. Tell him that the company appreciates his input and that he will be given credit for any constructive, practical suggestions.

How Paul F. Handled a Similar Problem

Paul F., supervisor of the maintenance crew in a metal products plant in Lansing, Michigan, was faced with some unhappy mechanics after his company reduced the size of their group when business was slow. He knew that Steve S., the ringleader of the crew and a chronic complainer, would be particularly bitter. But Paul had learned years ago how to get along with people who feel they are overworked. He made a point of giving a lot of attention to Steve. He never passed up an opportunity to express appreciation for a job well done or one completed under unusual circumstances. He tried to elicit suggestions and ideas from Steve and always gave them serious consideration. He shared information with Steve and with other members of the crew, a practice that demonstrated that he considered the craftsmen important team members. As a result of Paul's supervisory skills, his crew took the reduction in stride without making an issue of it.

During your career as a supervisor, you will undoubtedly encounter workers who gripe about increased workloads. You can curtail much complaining if you explain the reason for the increase beforehand and ask for each employee's cooperation. Almost everyone dislikes unexpected changes. If you give people time to think and prepare for a change, they will more readily accept it.

Often when people complain about how much work they are doing, they are simply asking for attention. If you satisfy that need, you'll have happier, more productive people working for you.

The employee who has a poor attitude toward the work rules of the company

The Problem

Tom H., serviceman for the sewing machine operators in a clothing factory in Chicago, feels that employees of the company should have considerable freedom in how they do their work. He has frequently been criticized for moving his fabric-supply truck too fast through the aisles. In order to avoid accidents in congested aisles, the company had set the speed for stock trucks to be no greater than that of ordinary walking. Yet Tom frequently moved his truck at a near run so that he would have more time for coffee and smoking after making his rounds.

Tom has also been criticized for not cooperating with other employees in seeing that the department makes its production quota each day, since it is his job to keep the sewing machine operators supplied with materials and clothing components. Tom has not made enough trips. The operators occasionally are out of material and sit idle until he makes another round of the machines.

When the operators complained to you, Tom's supervisor, about his delinquency, you asked him to make more trips, explaining why it should be done. You told him that no operator should ever have to wait for him to bring an item, and that he would be disciplined if that happened in the future.

Today you were called to the work area and informed that Tom had decided his job was "too taxing on his time" (his words to the operators) and that he would make a round only when at least two operators called to say they were out of material. And Tom had done just that a few minutes ago. You realize that you must act on Tom's behavior, but what should you do?

The Solution

Send Tom home immediately, telling him to report early the next morning to the personnel department for a meeting to decide what disciplinary action will be taken by the company. If Tom is a member of a union, tell his union representative of your action. Also, inform your personnel manager of the incident and the upcoming meeting. Then meet with your superior to discuss the situation and to decide what should be done about Tom.

You should suggest a one- or three-day suspension, unless company policy dictates otherwise. In view of Tom's behavioral record and your verbal warning about not causing operators to sit idle, your personnel manager may recommend much more severe discipline.

Many managers have found that delaying discipline until the next day enables them to better handle personnel problems. By taking a "cooling off" period before making a judgment, you can avoid the rash words and decisions that often result when your emotions are provoked by an incident. The postponement gives the supervisor time to gather facts and information from witnesses on what actually happened and possibly learn why it happened. The accused person has time to "prepare a case," possibly in conjunction with union officials. It is a certainty that everyone involved will be able to discuss the incident with a clearer head the next day.

How Company Policy Helped Another Supervisor Handle a Similar Problem

Walter W., a supervisor in a steel mill in Youngstown, Ohio, was informed of his company's new discipline policy just prior to the time it was made known to all employees. Supervisors in the plant had always had trouble with a few employees who continually abused the work rules concerning the wearing of protective clothing and the use of safety equipment. In view of recent legislation (of OSHA) on safety equipment, the company properly took the stand that such regulations had to be enforced and, if necessary, discipline would be meted out to assure compliance.

The new policy was based on progressive discipline to be administered in five steps. The first step called for the supervisor to talk to the employee about the offense and warn that another violation would not be tolerated. The second, third, and fourth steps consisted of suspensions of increasing length, varying with the seriousness of the violation. The fifth step was discharge. All disciplinary action, including the warning, was to be documented in the personnel files of the individual.

With a set company policy, Walter knew what to do when he observed one of his riveters working high above the ground without a safety belt. Walter talked to the riveter about the work rule, stressing its seriousness and the worker's safety. He then described and imposed the disciplinary penalty, making sure that the worker understood that this was not a personal decision on Walter's part.

The steel mill's disciplinary policy concerning work rules may seem simple, direct, and easy to administer, but the extent to which it achieves its objective depends on the supervisor. Would you turn your eyes the other way if you saw one of your workers, perhaps a personal friend, repeat a violation after you had talked to him about it a few days before? How many supervisors talk to their people about safety on a daily basis? How many rely on suspensions to make their point?

The company must have work rules in order to run the business, maintain control, and assure the safety of employees. It is your responsibility to enforce those rules.

The employee who has a poor attitude toward supervisors who are women

The Problem

"Buck" Rogers works as a dock hand at a large shipping terminal in Kansas City, Missouri. Buck comes from a family in which his father ran the home and made all the decisions concerning it, and his mother raised the children, did all the housework, and tried to please every member of the family. Buck had difficulty finishing high school and went without a job for a long time until he was hired just a few weeks ago as a materials handler and trucker at the terminal.

You are Buck's supervisor and you are a woman. You started with the company five years ago as a billing clerk. You've known all the drivers, dock hands, and warehouse people for years and you were readily accepted by them when the company promoted you to supervisor a year ago. But now you face a real challenge—you sensed it when you saw the look on Buck's face when he was introduced to you, you felt it when you gave him some jobs to do, and you overheard a remark he made to one of the other truckers: "Women should stay home taking care of the kids. This is a man's job." Since it is apparent that Buck doesn't accept you, you wonder if he might refuse to do a job you give him, or perhaps deliberately do it incorrectly and then blame you for giving him poor instructions. What should you do about Buck?

The Solution

Go out of your way to talk to Buck about the work so that he will get to know you. Once he learns that you handle the job no differently than a man would, you should be able to get along with him. Let him observe how you supervise other male employees. Discuss the job and work assignments with other men when he is present. Let him see that you are a capable supervisor and should be treated as such.

If you can arrange it without being obvious, *do* some of the work, instead of just directing. Try to pitch in when Buck and the others are very busy, so that you'll lighten their load and show that you can do a "man's" job.

If you have tried these ways to get Buck to accept you and after a reasonable period of time have failed, take a few minutes to have a talk with him about your position. Point out that more and more women are successfully handling jobs that at one time were thought to belong to men, and that you demonstrated long ago that you could handle this job. Tell him that the other male employees have accepted you and that you would like to know why he hasn't. Regardless of how he answers, you should see a change in his thinking shortly afterwards.

How Another Supervisor Handled a Similar Problem

When Betty M., supervisor in an insurance office in Chicago, was promoted to her job, she knew she would have to prove to some members of the department that she was competent and could perform just as well as, if not better than, a man. Before she accepted the job she had heard some of the men she now supervises say, "Women are too emotional," and "They use feminine ploys to get what they want." Resolving that she would not be guilty of either criticism, Betty tried to exhibit a sense of humor and to "grin and bear it" when male workers made unkind remarks. She realized that if she made an issue of such incidents, the remarks would probably become more personal.

Yet Betty knew that she would be making a mistake if she attempted to approach the job as a male supervisor would. Instead, she acted like a woman and won the respect of the entire group she supervised. She did this by taking a sincere interest in each individual and exhibiting kindness, intuition, tolerance, and friendliness. She accepted well-meant compliments simply and graciously, and disregarded petty remarks. If a man deferred to her, she considered it a bonus, but if he didn't, she would not take offense.

The many preconceived ideas and misconceptions about women supervisors make it hard for them to gain credibility and receive recognition for their work. One myth is that men don't like to work for women. The truth is that most men who complain about that have never worked for a woman. Another attitude is that women should stick to "women's" jobs. With extremely rare exceptions, most jobs can be performed by members of either sex. Tradition has led to classifying certain jobs as women's and others as men's.

Women in supervisory positions should act professionally. By being task-oriented and by not involving themselves with personalities they can successfully supervise both men and women.

The employee who has a poor attitude about avoiding waste and inefficiency

The Problem

"It is difficult in a machine shop to avoid waste." That's what Rick B., machinist in a large shop in the Gary, Indiana, area told you, his supervisor, when you questioned him about the large amount of scrap in the bin near his lathe.

Rick has been with the company for only three months. He had been hired off the street because the company needed more people to fill orders from the automotive industry for various machine parts. From the first day on the job, Rick has not been a skilled or conscientious worker. He has never really tried to improve his workmanship in order to reduce the waste he creates. He was overheard to say to a fellow machinist, "With all the money the company is making on these special parts, they can afford to have me slip once in a while on turning out perfect pieces."

You realize that you can't continue to accept the poor attitude, lack of skill, and the resulting waste and inefficiency of Rick. What should you do?

The Solution

It is apparent that Rick has some misconceptions about how much profit the company makes and how the skill and efficiency of the employees affect that profit. You've got to convince Rick that waste and inefficiency hurt the company and must be minimized. The best way to do this is to get cost figures on the material and parts that he works with and show him what one of his mistakes costs. You should also describe the overhead charges of the company, the cost of the equipment he is using, and the cost of maintaining that equipment. If possible, let him know just how much profit the company will make on some jobs, to show him that it is not excessive.

Emphasize the need for high-quality workmanship on his part. Point out that if a substandard part was shipped to a customer and caused an inconvenience, it could result in the cancellation of an order as well as the loss of future business. No company can risk that. Tell him that he is going to have to improve his performance or he may lose his job.

However, let him know that the company would prefer to have him stay on, and because of that you are going to suggest to management that he receive instruction and training. This might consist of a night class at a local trade school or an on-site training program conducted by either a company employee or an outside instructor.

After your conversation with Rick, see your superior to follow through with your promise.

How Bill P. Handled a Similar Situation

Bill P. is a new supervisor in a job shop in Philadelphia. His company provides various components to the aeronautical industry. Since much of the material the job shop produces is carefully checked and tested before being accepted, the workmanship has to be the best possible. The company constantly promotes a "no rejects" goal with its employees.

When Bill was hired, he was told there was a lot of waste and inefficiency in the shop and that he would be expected to make improvements. Soon after learning the job he began to look for solutions to the problem. He spoke to one of the sheet-metal workers whom he'd seen wasting a lot of material and joking about it. The man told him that he had given up the idea of trying to save metal long ago, and that he didn't care who knew about it. On further questioning, Bill learned that the man's attitude stemmed from a feeling that the company failed to provide adequate tools and equipment for the tinners to work with.

Checking out the man's story with other employees was easily done, and Bill learned that there was a lot of truth to the complaint. Bill soon convinced management to invest in new equipment. It wasn't long before the amount of waste dropped dramatically and the tin-shop employees became much more efficient and cooperative.

There are several reasons why employees sometimes have a poor attitude toward waste and inefficiency, and many of them can be traced to management's inadequacies rather than to the employee's bad temperament. Employees make errors and are apathetic about their work when there is poor communication with supervisors, when they're given old or improper tools and equipment to work with, when they are inadequately trained, and when they don't receive proper attention—all failings of management.

The employee who has a poor attitude about cleaning up and housekeeping

The Problem

The job of reactor operator earns the top rate of pay in a synthetic rubber manufacturing plant in Ohio, and John S. is a reactor operator in that plant. John successfully applied for the job a few months ago and has now been assigned to learn it. He seems to understand the procedures and work practices, but, as his supervisor, you have had trouble convincing John to keep the reactor work area clean and to pick up after himself, especially when chemicals have been spilled. When he's asked to clean up, John's usual response is, "That's not my job. The company has janitors for that type of work." What can you do or say to John to convince him of the importance of good housekeeping and the necessity of his participation in this effort?

The Solution

Every supervisor has to be a salesperson. Your task is to sell John on cleaning up and doing a good job of housekeeping by showing him that it's to his benefit. Your sales arguments should mention the high status and responsibility of the position of reactor operator. Emphasize that a job site that looks neat and well organized to visitors is a good reflection on the reactor operator.

However, perhaps the best way you can sell John on housekeeping is to point out the consequences of his not doing it. Talk to him about safety and fire prevention. Show him that good housekeeping makes a job safer because it eliminates most of the major causes of accidents and fires. Tell him that you're sure that he wants to be safe on the job.

Illustrate your words by giving examples of hazardous chemicals or slippery liquids on the floor. Everyone would want something like that cleaned up fast—no one wants to wait for a janitor to arrive to do it.

Point out that John has probably noticed that having the tools, scoops, and other equipment he uses handy makes the job easier. If each person didn't pick up and store such items after each use, working in the reactor area would become frustrating and aggravating.

What Dick K. Did about Housekeeping

Dick K. supervises the operators in the pilot plant of a large refinery in Houston, Texas. When he was promoted from operator to supervisor a few years ago, he realized that one of his responsibilities would be to see that the laboratories and development areas were kept clean. He had seen that this was a recurring problem when he was on the job as an operator, and he had an idea on how to handle it or at least make the job easier.

Dick talked to his superior about the problem and suggested that specific duties involving the responsibility for good housekeeping be written into the job description of each of the people he supervised. His superior agreed. When this was done and employees were notified, Dick encountered less resistance from those individuals who had previously felt that they shouldn't be expected to be concerned with housekeeping. By making housekeeping one of the requirements of the job, the company had emphasized its importance in running a safe and efficient operation.

Many companies today fail to recognize that good housekeeping habits improve the morale and productivity of the employees. Having work areas neat and clean makes work less tiring and can even promote creativity. Poor housekeeping, on the other hand, leads to mental fatigue—surroundings that are depressing can make the work seem more difficult and boring than it really is.

The employee who has a poor attitude about the security of company property

The Problem

Although you are aware of the necessity of keeping company property secure, some of your people may not be. Take, for example, your storeroom attendant, Paul S. He's been with the company a long time, but has never held a job involving much responsibility. Although he has been a loyal employee, he feels that he should be paid more for what he does because, in his words, "the company makes a lot of money and could afford it."

Since you supervise the receiving, shipping, and storeroom operations at your company, you are responsible for the security of the property and the material in these areas. Periodically you receive a disbursement record, which shows the number of items withdrawn from the storeroom during a given period. You've noticed that the figures for stationery items are frequently high—higher than they should be based on the number of storeroom cards turned in by office employees. Could Paul be either taking some of the material for his own use or permitting supplies to be removed without authorization? Should you talk to Paul about the situation? If so, what should you say?

The Solution

Paul should understand that he shares with you responsibility for the security of company property in the storeroom. Yet, you are unlikely to do yourself or your company any good by talking to Paul about the problem. An implied or actual accusation of theft is a serious matter; since you have no "hard evidence" that Paul is stealing company property, there is a real possibility of making a mistake.

The best way to handle this situation is to send a memo to all people with access to storeroom supplies. Point out company procedures related to operation of the storeroom and emphasize the seriousness of removing supplies without authorization. The memo should also describe what will happen to employees who are caught taking company property for personal use. It will be up to you, of course, to enforce the penalties when there is definite evidence of theft.

How Don F. Handled Supply Theft

Don F., supervisor for a toy manufacturing company in New York City, had a problem with employees taking company property home. Although the company didn't put batteries into its toys, it stocked several different sizes in the storeroom for use in testing the operation of the toys. Since Don signed all requisitions for storeroom purchases, he saw that battery usage was much higher than it should be. There was only one answer, especially when shortages were always greater during the holiday season.

Don took steps to remedy the situation. He posted a notice at the storeroom window that new batteries would be given out only in exchange for worn-out ones. He also purchased a large cabinet for storing batteries. It was equipped with a lock and located in the storeroom. Only the two storeroom attendants were given keys and they were told never to loan them. The usage of batteries at the toy company no longer was excessive after these controls were adopted.

Unfortunately, most businesses today have problems with the security of the company's assets. Employees at all levels, including management, continually face temptation in the matter of putting company property to personal use. The best way to handle such problems is by instituting good preventive controls designed to minimize theft, rather than by trying to catch those guilty of pilfering. It's always better to use controls, if you can. Persuasion may seem easier, but it doesn't always get the job done.

2

The Unmotivated Employee

The employee who lacks motivation is a constant concern to all supervisors. Whether the person does not like the job, dawdles at the work, seems to be simply lazy, or feels unappreciated, all such actions and feelings usually mean the person is dissatisfied and slow to cooperate. How can supervisors motivate these people? What should they do or say to get better performance? The answers don't come easily, because people are all different, especially in what motivates them. In the end, a supervisor just has to know what will motivate each person, and how to go about doing it.

The unmotivated employee who dawdles on the job

The Problem

Although it's often said that every office has at least one person who dawdles on the job, you hadn't thought much about the truism because you didn't think you had such a person in *your* office. However, when your boss mentioned last week that he had noticed some of your people hanging around, you suddenly realized that you *do* have a dawdler. It's Lois M., your billing clerk, the one who recently transferred to your department.

Lois has been seen fixing her nails or adjusting her hair at her desk. When she files reports and documents she is slow in finding the correct file and inserting the material. It's not a matter of her not having enough work to do, you've learned on investigation. There usually are quite a few bills in her "in" basket and her desk always is stacked with papers to be filed.

The work assigned to Lois is simply not getting done as quickly as it should. Also, she's making a poor impression on the boss and other employees who notice her. What should you do about Lois? Should the fact that she's been in your department for only a few months affect your decision? How do you handle a person who doesn't seem to have the desire to get a job done?

The Solution

Work pace is part of a person's personality and varies from one individual to another. Keep that in mind when you talk to Lois. Personnel studies of people performing various jobs have shown that they are most efficient when they work at their own freely chosen pace. The work pace that Lois has established for herself may be the best for her temperament.

Therefore, you must address the problem of the work not getting done. Avoid attacking Lois personally. Say something like, "Work is piling up on your desk and it has to be done to maintain office efficiency. Are you having a problem? Is there something we can do about it?" Continue by mentioning that such subjects are usually discussed during each employee's six-month performance appraisal, but that you felt it would be better if both of you talked about it now.

Tell her that her difficulty in getting the work done will hold her back when it comes time to consider raises and promotions. If she admits that she isn't very interested in the work, look for additional duties and responsibilities to give her, pointing out that her regular duties must still be performed.

Watch for a change in Lois over the next few weeks. The discussion may be all that was required for her to demonstrate that she can be more productive. If that's not the case, tell her that the work must be handled more efficiently and that if she can't improve, she should consider moving to another position, either in the company or outside of it.

The Action of Joe T.'s Supervisor

Slow workers are not uncommon in business and industry today, and a supervisor in a foam rubber manufacturing plant in California had such a worker on his hands a few years ago. The manufacturing process required a four-man crew in the pour area where molds were moved by conveyers through the various operations. Joe T., the youngest of the group, was unable to keep up with the pace that the other three men established. The men were paid on piecework basis, and the supervisor eventually had to replace Joe with a worker who could handle the job to the company's and the other workers' satisfaction. Fortunately, the supervisor was able to find another job for Joe where he could work at his own pace.

If you push some workers too fast, you can expect their efficiency to decline. Freely chosen work pace is usually more important to younger workers than to older workers. When younger workers set their own pace, they work much more efficiently. Older, more experienced workers, on the other hand, will more likely work at about the same efficiency whether they set the pace or someone else sets it.

If you have a person who is making errors and is working slowly try to find another job for him or her, one that will better fit his or her work pace. In all probability, the move will pay off—the person will become more efficient and will be better accepted by co-workers.

The unmotivated employee who seems lazy

The Problem

You are the supervisor of the laborers in the construction group in your company. The people in your group do hard, backbreaking work that involves hauling, shoveling, digging, and lifting. One of your people is Henry R., a middle-aged man from Alabama. By his actions, Henry shows that he dislikes hard work and avoids it when he can. Because of this, you must continually follow up on the jobs he does for you to be sure that they are completed properly. You have often found him loafing, and when you've spoken to him about it, he has responded that he was just "resting from the hard work." Is there anything you should do or say to Henry that will make him more productive?

The Solution

You've got to learn Henry's background and feelings if you expect to be successful in changing his habits. The best way to learn them is to take a personal interest in him. Ask him about his family and his hobbies. Learn what job he held before he started working with the construction group. Find out if he has any goals. Once you get to know him, you can formulate a plan for motivating him and getting him more enthused about the work.

Check up on Henry's health and well-being, too. Some people who give the impression of being lazy simply lack the energy to do much manual work. You may wish to have him see the company doctor or suggest that he see his family doctor. A possible answer to Henry's lack of motivation may be his attitude toward the job. Does he consider it very menial or degrading? You should always treat his work with respect when discussing it with others. Don't think that what you say won't reach his ears; it always does.

If you find that Henry is truly lazy, you must level with him. Point out that you feel he can do much more and be considerably more efficient, and that you would appreciate his effort to do so. Add that if he doesn't improve, you may have to replace him.

How John P. Handled a Similar Problem

John P., supervisor in a distribution center for one of the large frozen foods supply companies in Oregon, believes that most people are basically creative and constructive, and that they will work to achieve rewards and responsibility. As a consequence, he had no trouble in getting Butch W. to do a good job for him. Butch had transferred from the processing department to the distribution center and it was his "last chance" to work for the company. His performance in processing had been unsatisfactory and he had established a bad record of shirking responsibility and failing to do a fair day's work.

John's perceptive skill enabled him to see that Butch needed to feel appreciated and respected. John appealed to those needs by making Butch feel that he was part of a team and by convincing him that the team's success depended on all its members. John pointed out that if Butch did a good job, it helped not only himself, but others too, and that the people he worked with were counting on him, just as he was counting on them. Teamwork was essential in the distribution center because many of the operations were on a tight schedule.

Undoubtedly, part of John's success in motivating Butch resulted from his ability to convince Butch that nobody likes a man who continually lets you down. If you impress this on people, they will work harder in order to win the approval and respect of their fellow workers. The best technique for motivating people, especially those inclined to be lazy, is to make them feel significant. If you are not already doing this with your people, try it—it works!

The unmotivated employee who doesn't like the job

The Problem

Carl J. was a machinist in a Detroit shop. He liked his work and thought he had an easy job, but when the company automated some of its equipment, his job was eliminated. Desperate for work and unable to find a machinist's job, he hired on as a mechanic at a machine assembly plant.

The stress and pace of the assembly line are quite a bit different from working a lathe, and he no longer gains satisfaction from a specific achievement. Carl has begun to do as little as possible on the job and is often careless. Since he doesn't like his job, he is more of a handicap to the company than an asset. If you were Carl's supervisor and knew his background, what would you do or say to him?

The Solution

You've got to find a way for Carl to get enjoyment and satisfaction from his work. He will never be really productive until he likes what he is doing.

Upgrade his mechanical skill by arranging for him to get training in mechanical work. Test his aptitude for troubleshooting machine problems. Also, expand his responsibilities if you can. Try him on preventive maintenance jobs, work that is not geared to the pace of the assembly line. When you actually satisfy Carl's needs, he will be better motivated and more productive.

How Bob K. Handled an Unmotivated Worker

When Bob K.'s company discontinued a product line because it wasn't profitable, the company transferred workers to other departments. Most of the people were assigned to the service department where Bob was a supervisor. Much of the work performed was unskilled, and therefore it was a comedown for the people who were accustomed to doing skilled or specialized work. Pete T. had been an assembler of electronic instruments; he now delivered hardware from the storeroom to the various operating departments. The job was menial and did not present much of a challenge; consequently, Pete didn't like it.

Bob identified the problem early on and took immediate steps to prevent the company from losing a good employee. One of the first things he did was to ask Pete to suggest ways that the delivery service could be improved. Then he changed the title of Pete's job to "parts specialist." This move gave Pete more pride in talking about his work with other people.

Bob showed respect for the job that Pete was doing in conversations both with Pete and with the people receiving the service. Bob knew that no employee can be expected to like a job for which even the boss has no respect. And he made it as comfortable as possible for Pete to do his job by seeing that his delivery truck was always in good repair. Pete gradually took more interest in his work and contributed much to the company's productive efforts.

A 1971 survey by the University of Michigan's Institute for Social Research uncovered the factors that are most important to worker job satisfaction and motivation. The ones most frequently mentioned were: a knowledgeable supervisor who recognizes good performance and takes a personal interest in his or her people, an opportunity to expand the job, pleasant physical conditions, and work that requires skill, creativity, and new learning.

The unmotivated employee who is bored on the job

The Problem

Margaret K., an honors student in high school, wanted to be a secretary but was unable to find a job when she graduated. Needing work, she learned that your company was hiring parts assemblers in electronic equipment. She applied and got the job. You, as her supervisor, learned these things when talking with her a few weeks ago.

But Margaret is not happy with her work, which is highly repetitive. It wasn't difficult for you to come to this conclusion. The first few weeks on the job she made few mistakes and gradually became more productive with experience. But since then she has peaked and is sliding downhill. The quality as well as the quantity of her work is poor. She frequently forgets your instructions, seems inattentive to the job, and has become careless in handling some of the delicate material she works with. What should you do? You cannot tolerate such performance, because it is beginning to affect the quality and the quantity of the plant's output.

The Solution

You must first establish whether Margaret's problem is due to boredom or to a temporary condition brought on by trouble at home, a health problem, or some recent disturbing incident. Sit down with her and tell her what you have observed and learned about her work. Explain why her work is not satisfactory to you or the company. Ask her if she is aware that her contribution is below standard for the job.

Margaret will, in all likelihood, confirm that she is simply bored and will probably lamely reply that she will try to be more careful in the future. While you won't have a solution to your problem yet, you must make this your first step before you take any other action.

Boredom results from repetition. A person who follows the same routine day after day tends to become inattentive and careless, to ignore instructions, and to be unconcerned about quality. What's the answer to boredom on the job? There are four possible approaches: You can threaten to take disciplinary action, you can offer rewards for better performance, you can appeal to the person's pride, or you can provide variety or enrich the job. Each course has its advantages and weaknesses. Discipline usually has no effect, rewards and wage incentives have their limits, appeals to a person's pride have become "old hat," and requirements of the job restrict the changes and new methods that you can suggest.

To bring about a change in Margaret, you may have to try all these approaches, but increasing the decision-making part of the job offers the best chance for success. You can also encourage her to study other operations of the process and learn some of the other jobs. She might be of great value to the company as a "balance" person to fill in for absentees and people on vacation.

You will be better able to analyze the problem during and after your conversation with her. During that conversation, admit that the work is repetitive but point out how crucial it is to the company. Explain its importance and why it has to be done right. People become bored more easily when they feel their job is menial and noncontributory.

How Another Supervisor Handled Probable Boredom

Robert H., supervisor of the planners in an aeronautical plant in California, recognized that Larry B., the new technician joining his department, might soon be bored with his work. Larry was transferring from a research group that the company had decided to disband and had worked on a wide range of challenging problems.

Robert decided to train Larry by giving him a variety of assignments. He figured that diversity would keep Larry interested and motivated, thus staving off boredom. Using this approach, Robert accomplished another of his long-term objectives—by familiarizing the new member of the department with diversified jobs, he began training the person who might some day move into his job. No one currently on staff had the ability or willingness to do so.

Supervisors often are tempted to give their new people simple, easy assignments, figuring that the safest way to break in an inexperienced person is to minimize his or her responsibility (which also limits the amount of monitoring and supervision required). They believe that as the person becomes experienced, you can give him or her more complex and challenging work. The weakness of this approach emerges when the employee becomes bored long before the more difficult or challenging work is assigned.

The unmotivated employee who feels unappreciated

The Problem

Pierre has been working for you as a plaster-mold worker at a glove manufacturing company in southern Ohio for the past year. He had always been enthusiastic about his work, but now he seems to have lost interest. It shows in the pace at which he turns out new molds and also in his unwillingness to tackle new assignments. He remarked last week, "Do you really need this?" indicating to you that he doesn't feel his work is important.

Pierre makes plaster forms of hands that are used to make metal castings on which women's and men's rubber-coated gloves are formed. Most of the work is repetitive, except for brief periods after the company adds new styles to the line. Pierre works mostly by himself in the plaster-mold room, but in the last two weeks has been wandering around the other departments. One of the supervisors reported to you that Pierre was talking to a girl about looking for a job with another company. You don't want to lose Pierre since he is a good worker and the only plaster-mold worker you have. What should you do?

The Solution

You've got to rekindle Pierre's enthusiasm in his work, and the best way to do that is to show that you and the company appreciate his contribution. Make Pierre feel appreciated by letting him know that the company depends on his skill on the job, a skill that very few people have. Compare his job with some of the others in the company. Show him that his job is a key one in the company's manufacturing process.

Give him your full attention and show interest when he communicates with you. He will especially appreciate this if you can do it even when he knows you are busy. Keep him completely informed on all matters that may concern him, such as acceptance of his latest forms and upcoming changes being considered by management. By doing this you'll show that you are interested in him and his work.

Pierre will feel appreciated if you treat him with courtesy, dignity, and respect. Compliment him in the presence of others, particularly in front of people you know he respects. See that he occasionally gets a reward for job accomplishment. A personal letter from the boss or recognition on the company bulletin board are two of the many ways this can be done.

Pierre needs to feel independent. Give him a freer rein than he has had. Suggest that *he* design some of the forms, telling him that you're sure he has some ideas. Changes that make a job less confining—even ones that actually violate certain efficiency principles—may yield gains in productivity as well as in job satisfaction. Giving employees responsibility and opportunities for making decisions is very effective in helping them feel appreciated. Too often supervisors tell skilled people how to make something or what to do on a job without telling them *why* or giving them a chance to get involved in the job.

How Charles T. Handled His Unmotivated Worker

Charles T., supervisor of a cleanup and yard gang at a veteran's hospital in South Carolina, realized that a few of his people felt that the work they were doing wasn't important or appreciated. Bob J., in particular, had expressed dissatisfaction about handling the trash barrels and the garbage containers from the kitchen and about mopping the floors. However, some of the work that the crew did was pleasant and rewarding. The men enjoyed caring for the lawn and shrubs, and planting, cultivating, and cutting flowers.

Charles realized that he had to cut through the boredom and drudgery of much of the work to keep people like Bob motivated and productive. He decided that introducing variety was a way to do it. Charles knew that people like to know what jobs they are going to do before they come to work, so he set up weekly work schedules. Each Friday, a list of daily work assignments for each person was posted on the bulletin board for the following week. The work was varied as much as possible and spread equally among the crew members so that distasteful jobs were shared by all—and therefore were done infrequently by each worker. Bob and others were enthusiastic about these procedures and no longer complained when their day came up on some of the less pleasant jobs.

One of the best ways to encourage top-flight performance from employees is to introduce variety in their work—that will keep them interested as well as active. Active people stay motivated and feel better at the end of the workday.

Many employees become dissatisfied and unmotivated today because supervisors fail to provide a "human touch." People like to feel and *need to be told* that their work is important and that what they do is appreciated. When they can see the results of their efforts and know they are contributing, they become more satisfied.

When people demonstrate their competence at particular jobs, it's tempting to limit them to those assignments and forget about them. That way we don't have to worry about the work or about the people involved—or so we feel. But those we supervise would be much better off if we worked out a diversification program for them.

3

The Employee Whose Morale Is Low

The employee who has low morale usually is an unhappy and dissatisfied person. What's worse, this employee often promotes a negative attitude and feeling among other employees. When viewed in this light, the problem of low morale deserves the immediate attention of the supervisor.

Low morale is seldom hidden. You become aware of it by observing and listening to your people on the job. Typically, employees with low morale do their work reluctantly, are overconcerned with their safety, are excessively critical of supervisors and management, and complain that they are underpaid. The person who sees no future with the company is also suffering from low morale.

You and other supervisors can help with these problems, but you must be genuinely interested in the people and motivated to help them. Regardless of how you handle a specific problem, you will come to realize that there is much to be gained from improving on-the-job morale.

The employee whose morale is low because of on-the-job safety

The Problem

Bob J. is a welder for a steel products company in Pittsburgh. He is a meticulous worker and insists that his work area be kept neat and clean. As a member of the plant safety committee, Bob is very outspoken about safety. In fact, Bob feels that the company is negligent in providing safe working conditions for the employees. Yesterday he came to you complaining about the fumes at the welder's table where he does most of his work. He claimed that the exhaust system wasn't working properly. You immediately went to your superior and asked that the maintenance department check the system to see if the exhaust ductwork was plugged or if the fan was not operating properly, but the maintenance staff hasn't had a chance to work on the exhaust system yet. When you assigned a welding job to Bob this morning, he refused to do the work until the exhaust system is again working properly, saying that he is not going to jeopardize his health and safety. As Bob's supervisor, what should you do about his refusal to work?

The Solution

See that another exhaust system (portable) is immediately provided at Bob's work table or that the existing system is repaired before you again ask him to work there. A generally accepted rule on safety applies to this situation: If an employee feels that the condition under which you are asking him to work is unsafe, he has the right to refuse to do the work. Even when it can be proved later that the situation or work place was not unsafe, most arbitrators would support the employee's action. An employee should not be forced to work if he sincerely feels, rightly or wrongly, that he is exposing himself or others to danger.

Another way to handle this situation is to give Bob a job in an area where fumes will not be a problem; then follow up with the maintenance department to see why the system has not been worked on. You may have to ask your superior to help you if you can't get action.

If you don't have work rules restricting task assignments, you could ask Bob to work with a mechanic in determining what's wrong with the exhaust system and in correcting it. In this way, the problem is handled quickly and Bob will be working rather than sitting idle while someone else fixes the system. Also, Bob will learn what to do in case the problem comes up again.

Whichever course you follow, it is important that you trust Bob and respect his viewpoint. You are really being tested in this situation. Your future relations with Bob and his enthusiasm, cooperativeness, and respect for you as a supervisor depend on how you respond. A good supervisor is concerned with the welfare of subordinates.

After you resolve the fan problem, you should take time to explain to Bob that the company *is* very much concerned with safety. Even non-injury accidents cost money. The indirect costs of industrial accidents are several times as great as the direct costs (medical treatment and insurance). Indirect costs include time lost because of the accident, breakage, hiring and training people to replace those injured, management's time in making reports and investigations, work stoppages by other employees, and welfare costs. Management would be very remiss in its responsibilities if it didn't try to minimize such costs by providing safe working conditions for the employees.

How Another Supervisor Handled a Similar Problem

Tom B. has 15 years of experience in the production department of a gas generating plant in Oklahoma. Over the years he has become quite knowledgeable about safe and unsafe practices of employees—he understands the processes and the equipment in addition to having supervised many individuals. When the company hired additional people during an expansion of the plant's production capacity, one of the new men under Tom's supervision, Peter P., was quite concerned about safety in the plant, especially in his work area, the compressor room. He showed his apprehension by being overcautious in the tasks he performed and by asking Tom for impractical and unwarranted equipment changes and additions. Realizing that the worker was under stress, Tom quickly found ways to relieve it.

He persuaded Peter to become a member of the plant safety committee and to participate in plant inspections and accident investigations. He arranged for Peter to attend a safety conference and symposium in a nearby city, and he requested that the company's copies of safety magazines be routed to Peter. To convince Peter that the company's facilities and procedures were standard and safe in the industry, he arranged for him to visit another gas generating plant to see their operation. Peter continued to be an active member of the plant safety committee for several years, but after learning more about the equipment and the process, he no longer questioned the safety of his work procedures and the equipment he operated.

The apprehensions and fears of people on the job often stem from a lack of knowledge about the equipment and materials they are working with. You can minimize if not prevent such fears by seeing that people are well trained in the process they perform and familiar with the equipment they use before they are made responsible for it. This is especially true when they are concerned about safety. In addition, people who know their job well will perform it more safely and efficiently.

The employee whose morale is low because of low wages

The Problem

Kim R. is a typist and file clerk for an insurance underwriting company in Milwaukee, Wisconsin. The company has only 25 employees and you are the office supervisor. In order to hold down expenses, the president has kept a tight control on salaries and fringe benefits. Several of the people who work for you feel they should be paid more for what they do. Kim has been particularly adamant in this respect. Today she told you that she was going to look into getting a job with another company if she didn't get a substantial wage increase soon. You would hate to lose her because she is very efficient and a conscientious worker. How should you answer Kim's insistent request for more money? What should you do about the low morale in the office concerning salaries?

The Solution

First, find out whether Kim's pay is really below average for the type of work she does. To do this, compare her salary with what people in other offices are earning for the same kind of work. Call a local employment agency to describe her job in detail. You can do this for other jobs in your office too. If you learn that your company's pay policy is about the same as or higher than that of other companies, point this out explicitly to Kim and other members of your department. If the pay people are receiving is lower than that of their peers at other companies, you had better talk to your superior about what the company can do about it.

If the president refuses to increase wages, other compensations can be offered to deserving employees.

If the office doesn't have a small lounge or "break" area with coffee facilities and a refrigerator for the brown-bag lunches of employees, ask for one. You can tell the president, "Our people aren't making as much money as the people working for other firms for the same kind of work. If you provide amenities such as these, you can make up some of the difference."

Special treatment can often substitute for lower salaries. You might persuade the president to loosen up a bit by instituting weekly awards of tickets to the theater or ballgames, meals at a fine restaurant, or a day off with pay for an increase in productivity or the contribution of some special service. Awarding cash bonuses is another way for the company to show appreciation for dedication to the job. The yearly cost to the company of rewards or bonuses is much less than the cost of across-the-board pay increases. And even though employees may receive less money, the idea of prizes and bonuses is appealing. Periodic raises become routine in comparison.

There will be individual cases such as Kim's, of course, where all your efforts may be for naught; some desirable employees will find jobs that offer more money. When this happens, be gracious and don't hold a grudge. If you assure the employee that you'll provide excellent references and that the company will always welcome the person back if things don't work out, you can pave the way for a really valued employee to return to your company.

How Another Superivsor Handled the Pay Problem

Betty S., supervisor of a typing pool in a mail-order catalog sales company in Vermont, had a problem on her hands when Kathryn G., one of the typists, quit to take a higher-paying position with a new company that was actively recruiting clerical help. The problem was not that Kathryn would be sorely missed, but that other typists wanted to follow her lead. Betty was alert to the situation and came up with an answer. She asked each employee if she was willing to take on an equal portion of the work that Kathryn had previously handled, and earn an equal portion of the salary that Kathryn had been making. Betty told each woman that if everyone agreed to the plan, she wouldn't ask management for a replacement. She further explained that this was the only way she could think of to get more money for them because the department's budget just wouldn't permit any salary increases. When the typists agreed, Betty cleared the plan with her superior and put through salary increases for everyone.

The employee whose morale is low because of meager chances to advance

The Problem

José G. is a compounder in a large chemicals plant in Houston, Texas, that makes antioxidants for the rubber and paint industries. After two years of college, José was anxious to get out on his own and earn some money, so he applied for a part-time job between school terms. When he found that he liked the job and didn't want to go back to school, José asked to be hired permanently. Since he had applied himself well and the company needed a compounder, he was given the job. That happened five years ago. José is still on the compounding job, but now is discouraged because he would like something better and sees no chance to move up in the company. What advice can you, his supervisor, give him? Is there a way to bolster his morale?

The Solution

Find out what kind of work José would like to do so that you can determine what obstacles, if any, are in his way. Then tell him you want to help him to reach his goal.

Encourage him to complete his college education, either in chemistry, chemical engineering, or industrial engineering. Point out that the company is growing and will undoubtedly need people in research, development, and engineering in the future. Since he has done well in his present position, he would certainly be considered for one of those jobs.

Immediately look for a way to reward José for his good performance. Could he be promoted to senior compounder with an increase in salary? When an employee deserves recognition, the supervisor should see that he gets it promptly. Good employees are often lost because management is too slow to take action. A simple raise could very well make him feel that his present job has more status than he thought. You can justify a salary increase by giving José additional responsibilities and by changing his job title. He would see that he is achieving his goal of moving up to a better job.

José may be discouraged because he has become bored with the job or has been left out of the company's research and development efforts. If he does the same routine work each day, challenge him with some basic research problems. See that he is included in planning meetings. When employees are involved in the planning function, they will feel a commitment to carrying out the plans they helped to formulate.

If you feel José would make a good supervisor and would want the job, support him in an effort to fill one of those positions. That would give him valuable experience, and if he does well, it could eventually lead to a job in management. You can help him move in that direction by providing him with learning opportunities while he holds his present position.

The Solution to a Similar Problem in a Bank

The employees in the machine room of a large bank in downtown Chicago were mostly young people, some of whom had college training and were expecting to move up to higher positions. However, there was one exception, a woman who had worked at the same job for eight years. Angela M. hadn't finished high school, didn't learn as fast as the others, and wasn't as quick when it came to operating the machines.

When Angela told her supervisor, Barbara B., that she was discouraged because she'd never had a promotion, Barbara accepted the situation as a personal challenge. Barbara thought that Angela could handle the work in the loan department and would probably do a good job there because of her conscientiousness and empathy. Barbara told Angela that she would like to help her get a better job and would see that she had an opportunity to learn if she was suited to a loan officer's job, but Angela would, in turn, have to complete her high school education and then take a course in finance. The agreement was made and goals were set. During the next two years, Barbara provided encouragement and support, and today the bank has a much more efficient and happier employee working in the loan department.

Normally the personal life and habits of an employee should not concern a supervisor—except when the morale or well-being of the employee affects performance on the job. Then the supervisor has the responsibility to step into the situation.

When a subordinate's morale is low because his or her chances of getting a better job seem meager, you need to find out what kind of work the person would like to do. Then you can determine what roadblocks are in the person's way. If you take the trouble to learn how people really feel about their work, you can help them to adjust and improve themselves so that they have a chance at a better job. In doing so, you may also uncover the reasons for poor performance and can then make changes to bring about improvements.

The employee whose morale is low because of lack of confidence in management

The Problem

Ralph J. inspects uncured tires in a tire manufacturing plant in Tennessee. He has two years of college training in mechanical engineering but dropped out of school when his money ran out; he planned to work for a few years before resuming his classes. You recently told Ralph that with his technical ability and his experience in the plant, he might be able to get a job with the staff engineering group when he received his degree. But Ralph no longer seems enthused about finishing school. Moreover, he has begun to criticize management and the engineering department about the way some of the plant's problems have been handled. He thinks the competition is doing a better job of turning out quality tires and that many of the managers at the plant are incompetent. You sense that his expressed feelings may affect the morale and opinion of other employees. What should you do about Ralph?

The Solution

You need to sit down with Ralph to discuss his current behavior and his future. His attitude toward the company is counterproductive in that nothing positive is being gained and harm can come of it. Ralph's behavior is typical of a person who is frustrated, and you can understand him better if you recognize that. If you react to hostile behavior by striking back, you may make the situation worse. Start by accepting Ralph's behavior as natural for a frustrated person and by avoiding your own emotional response.

An employee's dissatisfactions and gripes are often inadequately expressed. A good supervisor brings them out in the open and confronts them. Discuss matters openly with Ralph. Disarm him with complete frankness. Let him talk it out, and listen to him. When dealing with frustration, don't depend on a single simple remedy; circumstances often exclude one approach but permit another.

Keep in mind that even chronic complainers sometimes have valid criticisms. Perhaps Ralph is the only one with the courage to tell you that the way the company handles lubrication of the machines is obsolete and inadequate. Maybe he's right. Listen to him, and ask solution-directed questions about the function to make sure you don't reach false conclusions about the validity or lack of validity of his criticism.

Regardless of what you learn about a criticism's soundness, make Ralph understand that he is jeopardizing his position with the company by casually criticizing management and by sharing his views with anyone who will listen. If he has a suggestion on how a procedure should be changed, he should come to you with it. Stress the effect his behavior could have on other employees' morale and on their attitude toward the company.

Depending on whether Ralph accepts your counsel, you may be inclined to go so far as to say that the company will not tolerate an employee's discrediting or running down management, and that if he continues to do so, he may be suspended or asked to leave the company. But remember that punishment and the threat of punishment do not deter destructive behavior caused by frustration; they increase it.

Encourage Ralph to make a turnabout, to get his degree, and to work toward joining the staff engineering group at the plant. Point out that if he were promoted, he could play a part in changing some of the engineering practice that he is now criticizing.

How Another Supervisor Handled a Similar Problem

Only a few months after becoming supervisor at a fabric mill in Gadson, Alabama, Carl K. learned that one of the people he supervised, Jason F., was telling other workers that management had made a big mistake in naming Carl supervisor, that Carl didn't know how to handle people. Carl felt he was doing a good job but he was aware that the people he supervised didn't have as good a production record as they had had under his predecessor. He talked about the problem with Andy C., one of the other supervisors and a man who he knew would level with him, to learn if there was any truth to Jason's accusation.

Andy made light of Jason's comments, yet made a point of saying that supervisors shouldn't try to be too demanding. Carl got the subtle message. He immediately tried to be less bossy and to let his people make some of their own decisions on the job, something he had not permitted up to that time. It wasn't long before the production record of his department improved—and soon Jason became friendlier and more cooperative.

When supervisors improve their techniques and learn how to get along well with subordinates, a more congenial attitude is fostered among group members. And a more satisfied and secure group is likely to accomplish more. It's important to both you and your company that you improve your leadership skills to gain the respect your position deserves.

4

The Disloyal Employee

Unfortunately, not all employees are loyal to the company they work for. They show their disloyalty in one or more ways, both on and off the job. Their action (or inaction) hurts the company as well as themselves. Supervisors must be on the alert for disloyalty and must act when they see or hear indications of it among their people.

You've got to know what to do about the person who talks down the company, who fails to keep a promise, who takes advantage of the company in work procedures, or who threatens to leave it. Loyal employees are concerned about their company, its success, and its future, while disloyal employees sometimes seem determined to destroy those things.

Many employees withhold loyalty until you and the company have proved yourselves worthy of it. As a supervisor, you must understand that you can't buy loyalty or win it with favors. You must build it by making people feel they belong and are part of a successful operation, and by having them understand that their success depends on each person doing a fair share of the work and cooperating with co-workers, supervisors, and management.

The disloyal employee who takes advantage of the company

The Problem

Alicia R. is a young technician with a plastics manufacturing company in Connecticut. She came to the company from a university well known for its excellent engineering curriculum. Alicia expected to start with the company at a higher level than the one she is at. Shortly after beginning work, she began to shun assignments that didn't require the use of her technical training. She also showed a reluctance to "get her hands dirty." Her disloyalty was reflected in the comment she made to one of the other technicians: "How the company does is not my concern. I'm interested only in work that will enable me to go into business for myself some day. I don't think much of the company, so I do only what I have to do." The other technicians in your department have begun to avoid Alicia; they prefer not to work with her on department problems, and vice versa. As her supervisor, what would you do about Alicia?

The Solution

Set up a time to talk with Alicia as soon as possible, because she certainly does not have the right attitude about her job and you cannot permit the situation to continue. Make sure her aloofness and un-cooperativeness are not due to a lack of understanding about what is expected of her or a disloyalty to the company. Define her duties and responsibilities and let her know you expect her to carry them out. If Alicia feels that some of the duties you have given her are beneath her dignity, try to convince her that this isn't so, but if she still feels that way, appeal to her loyalty to accept them. You might adopt a management by objectives way of handling Alicia to better control her performance, make her responsible for her actions, and see that she contributes more to the company's objectives.

A person's value on the job depends not only on talents and abilities but also on a willingness to use them in a way that will be most helpful to the employer. You must make this point clear to Alicia. Tell her that the most important requirement of her job is to satisfy the company to the very limit of her ability to do so. That was why she was hired. You could also insist that she spend part of her time in the production areas learning the operations and offering help when it could be used. Say that you are going to observe her actions during the next month and that you expect to see her working with other technicians.

Show Alicia that the way she is handling the job is hurting her as well as the company. When she shuns her peers she cuts herself off from an important source of knowledge and diminishes her on-the-job learning experience. Once she becomes a team member she will, in turn, get help from others on her projects, which is of course to her benefit.

Getting Alicia involved in planning may improve her performance and give her a different viewpoint toward the company. When people are involved in the planning function, they feel a commitment to carrying out the plans they helped to formulate. Alicia may find herself in positions where she will have to pitch in if the project she is working on is to go forward. If necessary, later on it would then be appropriate for you to keep the project rolling by saying, "Do you remember what we decided to have you do when you and I planned this project? Is there some reason why you haven't done it? Did you change your mind? Tell me about it."

Finally, set a date for Alicia's performance appraisal (no further than two months hence) to discuss her attitude and accomplishments.

How Charles P. Handled the Problem of Taking Advantage of Peers

Charles P. is a supervisor in the stores and receiving department of a large electrical supply house in New Jersey. The people who work for him receive shipments, fill shelves and bins with items, take inventory, and disburse merchandise. Since most of his subordinates have preferences about which jobs they do, Charles generally leaves job assignments up to the individuals, asking only that all the operations be manned and that individuals keep busy. This arrangement worked well for a long time; then two of the six members of the crew came to him with a complaint. They reported that Leonard R., one of the crew, seldom, if ever, helped unload trucks, the most distasteful job. Lenny either could not be found shortly after a truck arrived, or else promised to help when he finished his present task, which usually lasted until the truck was unloaded.

Charles saw that he would have to do something about Lenny, but he didn't want to talk to him for fear of disturbing the pleasant and cooperative arrangement under which the group worked. Instead he posted a work schedule in the receiving department that assigned dates on which two of the men would unload all trucks, thus dividing the work equally among the crew members. He prefaced the schedule by saying that he recognized that unloading trucks was a dirty, heavy job, and to be fair, he was dividing the work equally among members of the crew.

By handling the problem in this manner, Charles accomplished several objectives: (1) He avoided a confrontation with Lenny, which he was sure would amount to accusations and denials. (2) He recognized that it was his responsibility to see that distasteful work was distributed among all workers, with no favoritism shown. (3) He showed the crew that he was fair in handing out assignments. (4) He preserved as much as possible cooperative conditions under which the group worked.

The disloyal employee who fails to keep a promise

The Problem

Helen J., claims adjuster in an automotive insurance agency, is a key person in the office—her presence or absence determines how quickly claims are processed. Since the agency wants to handle claims as quickly as possible as a way of providing efficient service, you, Helen's supervisor, become concerned when she gets behind in her work. If the backlog of claims to be processed gets too great, you must make other arrangements to have them handled, a procedure that not only is costly, but also results in mistakes and unwarranted delays.

In recent months the situation has become aggravated by Helen's unexpected absences. You've talked to her about the problem and pointed out why it's important that she notify you in advance. Each time Helen has promised to call in the next time she was going to be absent. But she hasn't done so.

Today, Helen is again absent without notice. How should you handle the problem? What should you do about Helen's failure to keep her promises?

The Solution

Issue a written reprimand to Helen with a file copy for the personnel office. In the letter, inform her that if she fails to notify you of her next absence, she will be suspended for two days without pay, and that for the next similar offense the suspension will be for five days. Although she may fight this action, adopting a progressive discipline program is your most effective recourse. You may eventually have to recommend to your superior that Helen be replaced. If she belongs to a union, you should have no trouble with it—as long as you have discussed the problem with her and have followed up with written notification describing the suspensions that you will impose if the practice isn't discontinued.

Employees who are in embarrassing positions or are under stress sometimes make promises that they later decide not to keep. This is especially true when they realize there is no company rule holding them to their word. You may appeal to their loyalty and to their conscience, but you may only get another promise.

Nevertheless, it's always wise to give people a second and even a third chance before you take disciplinary action. If the matter turns out to be one of morale only and the individual has failed twice to keep a promise, you may as well start looking for other ways to handle the problem, such as by training a replacement. After you are sure a person understands the seriousness of the matter, follow through with disciplinary action at the next offense. You'll never solve the problem if you don't.

How Another Supervisor Dealt with an Employee's Failure to Keep a Promise

Henry R., supervisor in a printing shop in Dallas, Texas, heard via the grapevine that the practices of one employee were affecting the morale of other workers and were disrupting the operations in his department. Alan P. had been hired only a few months earlier but already had the reputation for being tight and money-grubbing. He took advantage of every "free to employees" or "discounted to employees" offer that the company made, and took home the greeting cards, calendars, invitations, and other forms the company made available to employees, whether he had a personal use for them or not. The word got around that he sold every item he could get his hands on. Because he was a new employee, people especially resented this.

Henry realized that he would have to do something about Alan's freeloading. When they discussed the matter, Alan apologized and promised not to take advantage of the company's liberal policy. But he didn't keep his promise, not even after Henry spoke to him a second time. Henry had to find a solution to the problem, but felt that discipline would not have a positive effect on Alan's behavior.

Henry persuaded his superior to request that the purchasing and production departments no longer hand out free or discounted samples without getting a slip, signed by the receiver's supervisor, entitling the person to be given or sold a specified number of items. With this procedure, Henry was now able to control Alan's freeloading.

The disloyal employee who criticizes the company

The Problem

Benny S., produce clerk in a supermarket, is now serving his third term as the union vice president. He is a very aggressive person who never hesitates to say what he thinks on any subject, including store management. He is strongly in favor of the rights of workers, and speaks out just as strongly against big business. He consistently finds fault with the company he works for.

When a new man was hired recently, you, his supervisor, were quite pleased with his initial attitude toward the job and with the way he handled the work you assigned him. But lately you've noticed that Benny has been advising him against developing good work habits. As a result, the new man performs considerably less work than before. In fact, yesterday you overheard Benny telling him to slow down and making a disparaging remark to him about management.

As supervisor of both men, what should you do? Should you talk to Benny, to the new man, or to both?

The Solution

Initially, talk only to Benny and do not mention his influence on the new hire. Benny is your immediate problem. You can try to undo his negative effect on the new worker later.

If you were to ask Benny how loyal he was to the company, he might wonder what you were getting at. He may not understand your concern; today, many people tend to think about the company's loyalty to its employees, rather than their own loyalty to their company. An employer is expected to show its loyalty by its willingness to help employees meet personal needs and by providing benefits such as life, medical, and dental insurance, pension plans, unemployment provisions, and tuition reimbursement, among others.

Ask Benny who supports the company. Explain that the company needs loyalty from the people who work for it. They should be concerned about its problems, its profitability, and its future. Loyal employees can make a company, and disloyal ones can break it, especially when the company deals with services to the public. If employees in a store are down on management and show it by doing only what they must do to get by, customers will soon be turned off. The number of people patronizing the store will drop and so will sales. In such instances, disloyal employees will eventually hurt themselves—they'll be asked to work fewer hours or may lose their jobs when they're no longer needed.

You need to look into Benny's attitude about the company. Most people are reluctant to be loyal to anyone until he or she has proved worthy of it. A person cannot be expected to be loyal to you as a supervisor or to the company unless you provide a good reason for demanding that loyalty. Has Benny been treated unfairly at some time? Can he give you examples of the company taking advantage of employees? Probe for the reason for Benny's disloyalty. When you learn it you can go about either proving to him that he has the wrong attitude or righting an injustice if one exists.

How Another Supervisor Handled Disloyalty

Paul B., supervisor in a recreational-vehicle rental agency, learned from a friend that one of his salespeople had been overheard talking down the company in a restaurant. Paul immediately called Kevin T., the disloyal employee, into his office for a talk. Paul explained that he had learned that Kevin had been criticizing the company in public about its rental policy and about the way business was managed. Paul followed this by asking Kevin whether the accusations were true. Kevin admitted that he had made a few such remarks, but that he had said them jokingly.

Paul told Kevin that all employees, especially salespeople, have to be extremely careful about what they say in public about the company. He added that if Kevin had any gripes about the way the company was run, he should discuss his views privately with Paul instead of publicly airing them. Paul's words had an impact and he never had to speak to Kevin about loyalty again.

If you find out that an employee is complaining about the company outside the office or plant, caution him or her about the practice. Explain why such behavior is dangerous and demeaning—not only to the company but also to the person who's complaining. Ask the disgruntled employee to come to you with any and all complaints.

The disloyal employee who threatens to leave the company

The Problem

Sid B. is shaping up as one of your most valuable employees, although he has been with the company for only six months. He was hired as a mechanic to repair equipment and machines in the metal products plant where you are a supervisor. Sid is a hard worker and is very ambitious. He understands equipment and is able to quickly diagnose a malfunction. A few weeks after learning the mechanic's job, he came to you with a suggestion that has saved the company hundreds of dollars.

Today Sid came to you and asked for a substantial increase in pay, despite the fact that your company has just announced that it is in the red because of poor sales and is actively trying to cut costs. Sid has informed you that he will leave the company if he doesn't get a raise. According to company policy, employees cannot be granted pay increases until they have completed one year of service, and Sid is not eligible for an increase for another six months. What should you do? Can you afford to lose Sid?

The Solution

First assess the situation to decide how serious it is. Is Sid's performance good enough for you to bypass company policy in order to hold him? Are you willing to replace him under present circumstances? What are your chances of finding someone as good as or better than Sid as a replacement? You must also think about the effect of Sid's move on other employees. He might persuade a co-worker to leave, and other people may get restless and start looking elsewhere.

There is no question that many employers take good employees for granted and often fail to appreciate them until it's too late. On the other hand, it is not uncommon for employees to leave a job for a year or two and then return. They may see that your company wasn't so bad after all, or that there were more opportunities for advancement with you than they had originally realized.

You should try to talk Sid into waiting a bit longer for his increase in pay. Explain company policy to him and remind him about present austerity efforts. Be sure to acknowledge his good work—assure him that management thinks very highly of him.

Before you resolve your position, consult with your superior to find out whether management is considering laying off people to cut costs. Because of Sid's short service, he could be one of the first to go.

How Richard J. Handled a Similar Problem— the Wrong Way

Richard J. was in charge of the machinists in a Detroit machine shop that provided service to the automotive industry. The business was very competitive, and quality workmanship was a requisite for survival. This was the reason that Bob T., one of the company's most skilled machinists, felt he could demand a large wage increase and threaten to leave if he didn't get it.

But Richard treated Bob no differently than any of the other machinists and postponed requesting an increase for him. After waiting for a reasonable period of time, Bob approached the company's closest competitor for a job and was promptly hired. The next day he gave two weeks' notice and let the name of his next employer be known.

When the notice came to the attention of Richard's boss, the machine shop manager, he immediately took action; he was quite concerned about losing a good machinist to a tough competitor. By offering Bob an immediate pay increase, he was able to persuade him to stay with the company. The manager also had a talk with Richard about recognizing and singling out talented people.

When you are lucky enough to have a few highly skilled or efficient people working for you, don't treat them like everyone else. They deserve special care and handling, the kind of treatment that lets them know their value and potential are being taken into consideration by you and the company.

Confront the potential problem of losing good people by planning what you will say or do *before* someone quits. You should know ahead of time the answer to such questions as: "What do I do if she leaves without notice?" "What action do I take if he goes with a competitor?" "Is there someone in the company who can step into the vacancy?" As you find answers to such questions, your plan will emerge.

5

The Employee Who Violates Company Rules

Violation of company rules has always been prevalent throughout business and industry. In order to combat it, many companies provide employees with booklets on regulations and procedures. Unfortunately, surveys indicate that such material is neither widely read nor well understood by workers—a booklet is a poor substitute for personal training. How should employees become acquainted with company rules? Their supervisors should inform them, preferably as soon as they are hired and start on the job.

When an employee breaks a rule, you must find out whether he or she was aware of it and understood the reason for the regulation. Overlooking a violation and saying nothing is equivalent to condoning it; in time, that could make a particular rule unenforceable.

You are responsible for seeing that chronic rule breakers are disciplined, either by you or by your superior. It is critical to remember that the purpose of the discipline is corrective, not punitive. Avoid sarcasm or threats, and never penalize someone without an explanation. Spend some time discussing the rule and clearly describe what you expect of the employee in the future. The person may be resentful, but not to the extent that he or she would be if there were no explanation.

The employee who violates company rules concerning attendance

The Problem

The attendance record of employees at the small lumber company you work for in Jackson, Michigan, is average for the area and the industry. You supervise 12 of the 15 employees. The company's vacation policy is liberal and is designed to offset the requirement that employees be on the job 6½ days a week. Two of your people have begun to be absent more frequently than they should be—and without good reasons. You are afraid that if you don't alter the situation other people will begin to take unauthorized days off and the attendance record will become progressively worse. What should you do about the problem?

The Solution

Your fears are well founded—it's important that you do something very soon about your two absentees before the situation gets worse or their practices rub off on other employees. Supervisors and management can solve attendance problems in several ways, but the key to each individual case is to learn *why* the habit has developed. Expect that each attendance problem you encounter will be unique in some respect; your corresponding solution must be unique for each problem.

Are the two offenders aware that the company expects them to be on the job every day, except when they are sick or have an emergency situation at home? Some people feel that the employer will overlook periodic absences. You must let all employees know that the company counts on their daily attendance. Point out that the company has provided additional vacation days that employees may use for personal business, and remind them that company policy allowed employees to take vacations in one-day increments.

Don't make it easy for healthy employees to be absent. Have them report to you personally when they return and ask for full explanations. Explain how much nonattendance costs the company in terms of production delays, overtime payments to workers who must fill in, and customer dissatisfaction.

It's a good idea to publicize an absence-control program and keep it alive. You can post individual performances on the bulletin board and provide rewards for good records. Don't give people a chance to forget that good attendance is important to you, to them, and to the company.

According to the Dartnell Institute of Research (*Personnel Journal,* January 1953), among 500 companies studied in a survey of absenteeism and tardiness, 30 percent reported rewarding employees with bonuses or prizes for being at work and on time, while only 8 percent punished infractions by making pay deductions. Not all the business world is so permissive—4 percent of the companies reported that they *discharged* employees for habitual absenteeism or tardiness.

Try to avoid using discipline to solve attendance problems—it should be your last resort. If an individual's absenteeism becomes excessive, look for deep-seated causes, such as alcoholism or drug abuse. However, when you encounter such a case, don't attempt to handle the problem yourself. Suggest to your superior that the employee be persuaded to see a doctor or a psychiatrist.

How Another Supervisor Handled an Attendance Problem

Wilson R., a supervisor in the painting and coating department of a metal extrusions plant in Youngstown, Ohio, recognized that Alex J. had a chronic problem with absenteeism.

On Fridays, workers cleaned and coated acid tanks, a dangerous as well as dirty job that no one liked. Wilson, therefore, kept records of which men did the work and attempted to distribute the assignment equally among workers. After a few months of following this schedule, Wilson noticed that Alex hadn't cleaned acid tanks in eight weeks—he had always been absent on every Friday that he would had been scheduled for the job. Wilson confronted Alex one Monday morning, asking why he had been absent the preceding Friday. When Alex offered a weak excuse, Wilson produced his attendance record and told him, "This shows a consistent pattern. It appears that you are deliberately avoiding the acid-tank job. If I let you get away with it, I may soon have other people doing the same thing." The record did it— Alex hasn't been absent on a Friday since.

Not all attendance problems are as easy to solve as this one, but you'll often find that if you let an employee know that you are aware of a "pattern" he or she is following, you have a good chance of bringing it to an end.

The employee who violates company rules concerning starting and quitting on time

The Problem

The maintenance department in your synthetic rubber manufacturing plant in Akron, Ohio, does almost all of its repair work during the day shift. Although the production process runs continuously, 24 hours a day, only a few maintenance and repair people work on the afternoon and night shifts. The production department wants maintenance people to arrive on the job promptly at 8:00 AM so they can make repairs that the night crew couldn't handle. You, as supervisor of the day shift maintenance crew, always hand out work assignments exactly at 8:00 AM so that work can start immediately.

But some of your people have been slow getting started. One fellow has a cup of coffee after you give him an assignment, another takes much too long to get his tools ready, a third always starts his workday with a leisurely cigarette, and many others can't begin tackling their assignments until they've finished discussing the previous day's sports news. You've noticed too that many of these same employees quit work early at the end of the shift. The company expects maintenance people to stay on the job until 15 minutes before the shifts change.

How do you go about getting people to do a full day's work? Should you discipline them by docking their pay when they aren't on the job as long as they should be?

The Solution

There's no question that you've got to do something and do it immediately. The present situation can only get worse. But keep in mind what your objective is: You want to change employees' behavior, not punish them for poor behavior.

To begin, talk with each offender privately. Point out that his shift starts at 8:00 AM and that you expect him to begin working at that time. Make it a personal matter between you and your subordinate. Avoid saying, "Management wants you to, . . ." or, "The production department expects. . . ." Most people won't buy such arguments— and some people couldn't care less.

If you have the respect of your people, this approach to the problem will probably pay off. You may have to repeat your message periodically, as a reminder. But eventually, starting and quitting at the right time will become routine.

If you are new on the job or have not yet earned the respect of your staff, you may have to vary how you bring up the subject from day to day. If workers do not promptly start tasks they have been assigned, try asking them if they need more information to do the work, if the job has been looked at, if your help is needed, and similar questions. Most people will get the point. Occasionally you may want to suggest that some fellows quit a few minutes early if they've worked hard or the day is hot. They will appreciate such thoughtfulness.

Some companies send employees a memo reminding them of specific rules and regulations when management notices a laxness developing. These reminders are usually not effective unless supervisors follow up by personally talking with employees. Docking a worker may be effective in some cases, but often causes the person to become belligerent and uncooperative, and to steal time from you in other ways.

How a Technical Supervisor Handled Late Starters

Julio E., supervisor of a group of technicians in a research department of a paint manufacturing company, combined a working knowledge of human nature with what he had learned in a psychology course to come up with a way to motivate some of his people. Recognizing that people would like to know in advance how their work day will be spent, Julio endeavored to tell them a day ahead of time what they could expect. Even though he could not do this every day for every individual, people generally started work earlier when they had time to think about it beforehand. Some employees began making preparations for the new work as soon as they learned of it and thus got a head start on the next day's assignment.

Whether you appeal to a person's conscience, rely on his or her respect for you, or attempt to motivate the person psychologically, it is wise to correct habits of starting late or quitting early as soon as you become aware of them. The longer you permit such behavior, the more difficult it becomes to change it. You should also try to avoid threatening people with diciplinary actions—you can't manage today's labor by threatening and intimidating.

The employee who violates company rules about proper attire

The Problem

Pete R. operates a punch press in a machine shop in New Jersey. He is an easy-going person who enjoys rock music and high-fashion clothes. Although the company furnishes coveralls for employees and recommends that they be worn on the job, dress is generally left up to the individual, except for those in one job classification. A notice is permanently posed in the machine shop forbidding machine and punch-press operators to wear ties or loose-fitting clothes.

Last week, Pete came to work wearing a shirt with large, billowing sleeves. You, his supervisor, objected, explaining that he was exposing himself to an accident—one of his sleeves could very easily be caught in the moving machinery. You also reminded him of the company rule regarding this and expressed surprise that he had forgotten it. Reluctantly, Pete took off his shirt and wore one of the company coveralls during the time he operated a machine.

Today, Pete came to work with a long, free-flowing sash for a belt. This time he would not remove it, claiming that at waist level and below, clothing would not get tangled in the machinery. He removed it only when you refused to let him work unless he did so. You are sure he is not going to give up his crusade to dress as he pleases, and that some day soon he will again violate the company rule. How should you handle Pete and his aversion to come to work properly dressed for the job?

The Solution

You, representing management, are very much within your rights to refuse to let Pete work if, in your opinion, he is dressed unsafely for the job. If he questions your authority, suggest that he submit a grievance so that a ruling can be made at a higher level of management. But do not let him risk an injury while the grievance is being processed.

If Pete refuses to dress properly for the job and also refuses to wear the company clothes, you may have to suspend him for a day or two. This should certainly communicate to him how serious the matter is. However, suspension should be a last resort. Tell Pete you don't want him to have an accident and you're sure his family feels the same way. Describe any actual accidents involving ties, rings, key chains, and so on. State that these accidents could have been prevented if people had dressed properly.

Many companies, particularly those in hazardous industries, require employees to wear fitted, company-furnished uniforms when they are on plant property. In addition to helping to prevent accidents with machines and equipment, uniforms also protect employees from skin exposure to chemicals and dust, and when the clothing is fireproofed, additional protection is provided.

How Another Supervisor Handled a Dress Problem

Lon S., supervisor in a potato chip and pretzel plant in St. Louis, is well aware of the strict health, sanitation, and safety requirements in the food industry in general and in his company in particular. Workers are required to wash before starting on the job, and clean uniforms are provided daily. Hair nets are supplied to employees whose hair is longer than a specified length.

A problem arose when the company hired Sal, a young, individualistic repairman, to maintain and service the company's mixing equipment, conveyors, and ovens. Sal's long hair hung in curls that fell to his shoulders. When Lou told Sal he would have to wear a hair net, Sal strongly objected, saying that men working in the office had long hair like his and didn't have to wear nets.

Lou explained that the office workers didn't come in contact with the products, therefore they weren't subject to the same health and sanitary regulations. Although Sal continued to argue for some time, he eventually accepted Lou's order when he was told that he would have to conform to the rule or find himself another job.

The employee who violates company rules regarding safety

The Problem

A sign prominently posted on the door to the laboratory of the cements and adhesives company you work for reads *"No Smoking at*

Any Time." Similar signs can be found in other areas of the plant where volatile hydrocarbons are processed, tested, or stored. Using bulletin boards and safety booklets, management has publicized the danger of fires or explosions that could result from smoking in such areas. Everyone knows that smoking in the plant is limited to the office area and the cafeteria.

This morning the laboratory manager called you to say that he had found one of your subordinates, Pete C., smoking in an isolated back area of the laboratory. When confronted, Pete didn't deny that he was smoking, but said that he felt "it was safe because nobody was working back there."

The people you supervise in the service department are permitted to smoke in the office and the cafeteria during their workday. Pete was probably delivering material to the laboratory when he decided to have a smoke. What should you do about the incident?

The Solution

Recommend to your superior that Pete be suspended without pay for at least a week. Also, warn him that immediate dismissal will follow if he is again found smoking in a restricted area. Your superior may wish to impose even stronger discipline depending on how management views the seriousness of the offense.

A supervisor's first responsibility is to take whatever measures possible to safeguard the health and welfare of employees. Pete's smoking could have caused an explosion or a serious fire; his action jeopardized the safety of everyone in the plant.

Pete may feel that suspension is too harsh a penalty for a first offense and may fight your decision. Make sure he understands that "no smoking" rules are different from other company rules—offenders may not get a second chance. The damage that could result from breaking a "no smoking" rule is much greater than from breaking other rules.

Very few companies are lenient with employees who violate safety rules. The costs of accidents, both direct and indirect, are well publicized—because they are so great. Unions almost always will support management in the enforcement of safety rules.

How Another Supervisor Handled a Safety Problem

Larry B., supervisor in a refinery in Gary, Indiana, worked for a company that rigorously enforced all safety rules. In the hazardous refinery industry, extreme precautions are required to prevent fires and explosions. One of the duties of Chuck B., a recovery-process operator working for Larry, was to measure and record the vapor concentration of a still with an explosion-meter. One day, Larry noticed that Chuck had become negligent about recording his measurements and called Chuck's attention to the lapse. Chuck assented that he had made the test and the vapor concentration was within a safe range. Larry told him that the job involved reporting the level on a form and that he had better not forget to do it again.

At the end of the shift, Chuck had still not recorded any of his measurements. Larry drafted a letter to him, reprimanding him for violating the work rule and for refusing to obey orders. A copy of the letter was entered in Chuck's personnel file. In an attempt to maintain a clean work record, Chuck filed a grievance saying that the violation was a minor technicality. The company's answer was that operators knew that all safety rules are enforced without exception at the plant. An arbitrator was given the case and ruled in favor of the company, stating, "Safety is of the utmost importance. The company's judgment in imposing discipline for breaching safety rules should not be lightly disturbed."

Although it's true that the law places a heavier responsibility on the employer than it does on the employee when questions of safety and health are concerned, the employee is required to be cautious and careful. If the employee persists in unsafe behavior, dismissal is a logical course of action.

6

The New Employee

A major responsibility of all supervisors is to start new employees off on the right foot. Both the employee and the company benefit when orientation is handled properly. Some companies recognize that a new employee's first few days on the job are critical ones and offer help and guidance, but others adopt a sink-or-swim attitude. In either case, many varied problems can arise that the new employee's supervisor must handle.

Problems exhibited by new employees include: poor personal habits on the job, objections to company rules, lack of interest in the job, general inexperience with the work, and an inability to adjust to the job within a reasonable time. These problems are not insurmountable—a good supervisor attacks them as soon as they are apparent and helps the employee to solve them.

The new employee who brings poor personal habits to the job

The Problem

Nancy K. is the new sales engineer hired by the customer relations department of a large oil company with central offices in New York

City. She previously worked in a small office for a family-owned automobile agency and is familiar with the usual office operations and sales functions.

You, Nancy's supervisor, have assigned her to work with one of your experienced sales engineers for training. She appears to be learning fast and may soon be ready to solicit and handle new accounts by herself. Certainly she has the self-confidence and educational background to enable her to do the job. But she also has some personal habits that bother you.

Nancy regularly comes in late. In addition, she has been spending a lot of time on the phone—obviously on personal business. And she spends too much time, in your opinion, smoking in the women's lounge. How should you handle Nancy? Should you criticize her personal habits?

The Solution

Although you might say something to Nancy now about her tardiness, it would be better for you not to bring up the other undesirable behavior until her training has been completed. The engineer who is training her may not have kept her busy enough to occupy all her time. After she is on her own and has adjusted to the new job, she may be an entirely different person.

Problems can arise when a new employee is confronted about personal habits by a supervisor. Fear of management and a feeling that management is too demanding can turn a new employee off. The result is an unmotivated person who does only what is required, who will follow all instructions literally.

An employee who feels personally put down may simply quit. New employees are more likely to take this step than old employees, because they are in the process of asking themselves, "Will I like this job?" and "Can I work for this supervisor?" Also, criticism of personal habits may be the last straw for a person who does not need the job. You can't get a person to willingly behave better by using negative, unconstructive criticism.

Supervisors need to make sure a new employee has enough to do. Nothing is more frustrating to a person on a new job than to have to find something to do or to kill time on "busywork." You can get a new employee to adjust a lot faster and avoid adopting poor personal habits by giving him or her a challenging assignment as soon as you see that it can be handled.

How Another Supervisor Handled
Poor Personal Habits

When John K., supervisor of the inspectors in a toy factory in Buffalo, New York, learned that the company was going to increase the size of his group in order to improve the quality of products, he immediately asked where the new inspectors would come from. He knew that management would be closely watching the productivity as well as the efficiency of the new inspectors as a measure of the wiseness of making inspectors out of employees now on other jobs. John also realized that, rather than hire new people, the company would transfer some present employees in order to take advantage of their knowledge and experience with the manufacturing process.

After learning the names of the people who would become inspectors, John talked to their supervisors, asking about the type of work they did, how they got along with other employees, and what personal habits they exhibited. He thus knew quite a bit about them before they joined his group. With this information, John was able to plan the orientation and training of each person so that any bad personal habits could be deterred before they became firmly established.

Any time you as a supervisor have the opportunity to get advance information about a new employee, take advantage of it. You will be in a position to do a better job of training, to prevent misunderstandings, to clarify rules and regulations, and to enable the new employee to more easily adjust to the job.

The new employee who doesn't seem interested in the job

The Problem

Elmer T., the new salesperson who started to work for you last week selling hardware, has little sales experience, having been a carpenter for many years. However, your firm in Chicago is a large one and handles a wide range of products. Elmer's familiarity with tools and construction materials should serve him well on this new job. Yet after eight days on the job, Elmer doesn't seem interested in his work. He frequently talks about carpentry and the satisfaction of completing a project. Although you introduced him to other salespeople, explained company policies and procedures, and showed him the products he would be selling, he lacks the enthusiasm necessary to get started and make a sale. For example, he prefers to let other salespeople take phone calls, and seems reluctant to talk to customers. The company needs salespeople at this time, so you would hate to see him quit. What should you, his supervisor, do about Elmer's lack of interest in the job? How can you motivate him to sink his teeth into the work?

The Solution

The dissatisfaction and sometimes early departure of newly hired employees can often be avoided by good communication—and lots of it—during the critical first days on the job. You may not have communicated well enough with Elmer. He is reliving his former job instead of learning and thinking about his current one. You need to fully describe the nature and duties of the job, because unexpected responsibilities might confuse or alienate him. Failure to completely explain company rules can cause misunderstandings. Even if you've handled these matters, taking the time to go over them again with him will show him that you are interested in him and how he does on the job.

Elmer has the potential to be a good salesperson for the company; it's well worth your time and effort to help him succeed. When he was offered the job, he was probably treated like a VIP—because the company needs salespeople, interviewers probably made an effort to impress him. Elmer most likely reported for work with high expectations. If his first few days didn't live up to those expectations, then his ego and morale may well have been deflated. A big buildup will only lead to a big letdown if people treat him as if he's part of the hardware once he's on the job.

There's a strong possibility, too, that Elmer is not an extrovert and doesn't have the aggressive nature typical of salespeople. But that may come with time and experience. Elmer needs to feel confident that he can do the job. He also needs to believe that you have faith in his ability to succeed.

Sharp supervisors, no matter how busy they are, don't handle new employees in a mechanical or routine manner. They give people personal attention, they schedule time to orient them, and they assign them jobs they can handle during those critical first days.

How Supervisor Tracy H. Handled New Employees Who Weren't Interested

The turnover of people in the machine room of a bank in Philadelphia was quite high, and Tracy H., the supervisor, began searching for the reasons. She found that many of the workers lost interest in the job very quickly. Tracy took steps to correct the situation.

After observing and talking with employees new to the department, Tracy saw that they were all anxious about their new jobs and were asking themselves, "Will I like the work? Will I be able to handle it? Will I be accepted?" Knowing this, Tracy worked out a plan, and when the next new employee arrived she was prepared to act. She provided information and guidance, encouraged the employee to ask questions and to talk about some of her concerns, and tried to put her at ease. Tracy also assured the new worker that the job would be interesting as well as satisfying. And she encouraged everyone in the department to help others with the work so that nobody would become bored doing the same job.

But that wasn't Tracy's entire attack on the problem. She showed her continued concern by periodically checking on how each person was adjusting and progressing. When Tracy's personalized approach reduced turnover, she demonstrated to herself and to the company that the best way to maintain a new employee's interest in the job is to maintain an interest in him or her.

The new employee who is inexperienced

The Problem

Lisa M. is a young girl who was transferred to your department last week to fill a vacancy in your typing pool. She had previously worked as a switchboard operator, but that job was eliminated when the company installed a new telephone system. Since she had some typing experience, the company offered her the job in your department as an alternative to being laid off (there were no other vacancies for which she was qualified at the time).

It is evident to you that Lisa has had very little typing experience; she is not improving with on-the-job practice and seems out of place in the pool. What should you do about the situation? Of course, you must talk to her about her performance, but what should you say?

The Solution

Inexperienced employees are often not aware that they are doing an unsatisfactory job. Your first step in Lisa's case is to ask her if she knows that you expect her to do a better job in the typing pool. What she says will tell you how the two of you might solve the problem.

If Lisa is a conscientious person and wants to improve her performance, she may readily agree to take a typing course in the evenings, either at her expense or at the company's, if the company provides tuition assistance. If she doesn't voluntarily agree, you may have to insist that she get such training by making it a requirement for holding the job.

Lisa may have accepted the job on a trial basis to see if she liked the work or if she could meet the requirements of the position. Your discussion with her could prompt her to accept a layoff and to notify the personnel department that she would like to be considered for the next job opening that she would be qualified for.

An inexperienced worker puts a burden on his or her supervisor; such an employee is more likely to have an accident and is not as productive as co-workers. Almost every person who is inexperienced requires training.

Supervisors play key roles in helping inexperienced employees to adjust to new jobs; supervisors must train new workers until they become skilled and productive on the job. How quickly they adjust and how adept they become depends a great deal on the abilities and patience of their supervisors. You as a supervisor are a greater asset to your company if you are a good teacher and trainer.

How Robert W. Handled Inexperienced People

Robert W., supervisor in the employees' activities department at a large greeting card company in a suburb of Chicago, recognized that his responsibilities to the company increased each June. For a long time, the company had provided summer jobs for some of the sons and daughters of employees. These inexperienced people came under his supervision, as most of the jobs consisted of maintaining and servicing the various recreational facilities at a lake and park belonging to the company.

Because Robert usually had new people to work with each year and the jobs were quite varied in nature, he realized that he needed an organized system to handle the summer employees. He therefore prepared a detailed description of each job. He also requested that the personnel department provide booklets giving facts about the company, policies, and rules of behavior for employees. Each new employee's first day on the job was spent entirely in indoctrination and training, regardless of how simple the job was that he or she was assigned.

Through Robert's efforts, the inexperienced employees whom he supervised quickly adjusted to their new jobs, found it easy to get along with other employees, and got satisfaction from their work. The company also benefited in having temporary employees who appreciated what the company was doing for them, performed their work safely, and were more productive than they would have been without Robert's supervision.

How you as a supervisor handle inexperienced new employees is a good measure of your management abilities. It's a big responsibility, one that justifies much time and effort. Be assured that these employees will long remember what you do for them.

The new employee who doesn't adjust to the job

The Problem

You are the supervisor of the visual display department of a large department store in New York City. Cheryl T. came to work for you a few months ago when her job in the advertising department was eliminated. The personel department felt that Cheryl would be a valuable addition to your group, particularly since the work would be quite similar to what she had been doing.

Cheryl had been an art major at a nearby university. On the job she had provided many of the sketches and illustrations used in the company's advertising. She was well thought of by management. But Cheryl is not meeting your expectations of her. She often disagrees with you about how scenes should be depicted, what kind of background props should be used, and even how various types of clothing complement one another. Moreover, she seems to want to take over when it comes to presenting new ideas on how merchandise should be displayed in the store. How should you handle this newcomer who isn't adjusting to the job the way you think she should?

The Solution

People whose personality and performance suggest a good future with a company are relatively rare, particularly if they are well educated and have relevant professional training and experience. Such high achievers often are difficult to manage and are a perplexing problem to their supervisors.

The answer in Cheryl's case is to manage her as little as possible. She has demonstrated that she will not respond to the traditional management techniques of authority and control. You will have to adjust to her—and you can probably do that faster than she can adjust to you. Cheryl should be handled as a gifted individual. Approach her in a way that gives her maximum opportunities for self-expression. You have, in Cheryl, a person who motivates herself. She is not easily manipulated, but that should not be of major concern to you. In her own way, she is probably capable of contributing more to successfully carrying out the functions of your department than any other member of your group.

Highly creative and exceptionally talented people sometimes bother their supervisors—they appear to challenge authority. Usually they are simply expressing their independence. If you go along with them and give them as free a rein as possible, you'll get the most out of them.

When a new employee begins a job doing work that is very similar to what he or she had previously been doing, there is often a smoother transition to the new job than you might think possible, especially if the person is a confident, secure individual. The individuality and the spark that the person brings can be an asset to the department and the company.

How Another Supervisor Handled a New Employee's Adjustment

When Harry P., supervisor of the materials handling department of a building supplies firm in El Paso, Texas, heard that the company had decided to hire an industrial engineer for his department, he knew that the responsibility for getting Joel off to a good start was up to him. Fortunately, Harry had interviewed Joel during the hiring process and therefore knew something of his background.

To prepare for the new engineer, Harry listed the various training steps he would take, planned a complete tour of the firm's facilities, and arranged for introductions to the people Joel would be working with. He made sure Joel's office was well equipped and selected the work projects he could assign Joel, based on his known capabilities. After Joel was on the job, Harry followed up each morning for the next couple weeks by talking with him about the previous day's experiences and asking if Joel had any questions.

Since he knew that Joel would be given challenging engineering problems as soon as he demonstrated he could handle them, Harry wanted to ensure Joel's fast adjustment to the job. And that's just what he got—largely because of his methodical preparations. A supervisor who is too busy to properly orient new people personally will be even busier trying to undo the trouble later.

The new employee who objects to company rules

The Problem

Blair J., a technical writer, came to the corporate training department of a large electrical products firm in Schenectady, New York, from a journalism school in the Midwest. You, her supervisor, have been training her on the job for the last two weeks. Her work will primarily consist of writing specifications and manuals.

Blair appears quite capable of handling the editorial aspects of the job; she has had experience working on the editorial staff of the university newspaper and also worked for a public relations firm part time between semesters. She is having difficulty, however, adjusting to the office routine of starting work at 8:00 AM, taking only 45 minutes for lunch, and staying on the job until 4:45 PM. At the public relations firm, her working hours were much more flexible. Your company provides a cafeteria for employees who don't carry their lunch, but Blair has persisted in leaving the building to eat at nearby restaurants. Several times she has been out for more than an hour. When you talked to her about this, her response was, "What difference does it make if I get my work done?" What should you do to help her to conform to the work schedule and rules of the office employees?

The Solution

This problem is different from the first one in this chapter, where Nancy K. was in training and company rules had not been discussed at length with her. The solution to the problem is accordingly different.

Many young people find it difficult to accept the regimen of strict office hours imposed on them by their companies. Blair is typical in this respect; some of your company rules seem to her to be trivial or unimportant. Regardless of how she views them, though, she must abide by them or expect to be disciplined. New employees, especially young people, should be made aware of company rules and procedures as quickly as possible—the first day on the job is not too soon.

Take the time to talk to Blair about why the rules are necessary. Mention that some employees may break rules when they believe they will not be punished for doing so, but that you believe violators should be disciplined. There would be no order if this were not done.

Supervisors are most effective when they treat each new employee as an individual. Begin learning about each person's interests the day he or she starts working for you. Get the person to talk about his or her goals or ambitions. Never make fun of an unexpected remark. It is discouraging and irritating and can undo weeks and months of on-the-job coaching.

New employees must see how following the rules pays off. Show them how it's helped others get ahead, built job security for them, and enhanced the satisfaction received from their work. Explain how learning new jobs or different methods makes the work more interesting. When they see you are right, they will be less inclined to go their own way.

Supervisors should always try to win new employees over to their point of view on company rules. If supervisors can't do that, their only recourse is to make sure that the new employees understand that offenders will be disciplined—an action that the company does not like to take.

How Another Supervisor Handled a New Employee

Milt C. is a lift-truck operator who works for a motor freight company in southern Ohio. He had previously worked for a construction company where the few work rules regarding employee behavior on the job were largely ignored. As a result, Ron, supervisor of the operators, saw that he had a serious problem to contend with the first day Milt started work. Milt could not understand why drivers were not permitted to smoke while working, objected to the governors put on the lift trucks to restrict their speed, and was disgruntled to learn that he would not be paid for days he was absent.

Ron realized that Milt's first few days on the job had to be carefully managed. He decided that with Milt he would need to establish his authority immediately and make clear how jobs are handled and what rules are to be followed. Consequently, he took the entire afternoon to talk with Milt about safety, company policy, and work rules affecting operators. He made sure that Milt understood he would be disciplined if he violated the rules. This talk had a sobering effect on Milt and he came to work the next day in a much more cooperative and agreeable state of mind.

Incomplete and misunderstood company policies can cause poor morale, unintentional violations of fair employment and safety laws, high employee turnover, and dissatisfied employees, all of which cost your company time and money. In many companies, the personnel or training department informs a new employee about employee functions, benefits, and activities. Although this induction may be valuable and informative, it won't help the new employee half as much as an informal person-to-person chat with you, the supervisor.

7

The Older Employee

Advancing age affects each person differently, depending on that person's physical condition, heredity, living and working conditions, eating and drinking habits, and emotional and psychological makeup, among others. You can expect signs of change due to age when employees reach 50 to 55 years of age.

The problems that can arise with older employees include poor health, diminished interest in their work, decreased performance, loss of ambition, and resentment toward young people. Supervisors can deal with these problems in a variety of ways but should always show respect for older workers. Remember, offsetting those drawbacks is a wealth of knowledge and experience, assets that all companies need.

The older employee whose performance has fallen off

The Problem

Brian W. has almost 40 years of service with a large automobile plant in Pontiac, Michigan. For the last five years, Brian has been under your supervision in the motor division. Brian has always done mechanical work of one type or another; most recently he has been putting together motor components on an assembly line. Although much of the work has been automated, he is constantly on his feet, rigging and moving heavy parts with hoists. You've noticed that lately he sometimes has trouble keeping up with the moving conveyers and that he sits down at every chance he gets. Unassembled motor components get past him more frequently today than they did a year ago, and another mechanic often has to help him. The quality control people recently have reported that some of his work will not pass inspection. What should you do about Brian? His performance has fallen off too much for you to permit him to continue doing the job in this manner.

The Solution

An employee is entitled to a job as long as he or she can perform all the requirements of it according to established standards. Age alone should not be a criterion for taking a person off a job. However, when an older employee cannot perform tasks satisfactorily because of physical or mental disabilities, the supervisor faces a dilemma. Every supervisor has a responsibility to the company to maintain a high standard of performance, but he or she also has a responsibility to the employee who has served the company loyally for many years and made a worthwhile contribution.

Nobody would enjoy telling a worker like Brian that he is not doing his job well enough and that something will have to be done about it. But that's an obligation that you, as his supervisor, cannot avoid. You must talk to Brian about the problems created by his diminished productivity and efficiency. Although the company owes a debt to Brian for serving it well for many years, Brian should recognize that the company must continue to operate and that it cannot permit productivity to decline in any area because an employee is unable to keep up with the work. Don't be surprised if Brian is aware of his failing on the job. He may even welcome the opportunity to discuss it with you. Both of you will likely feel better after talking about it.

There are a number of options for you to investigate in Brian's case, depending on company policy, agreements with the union, and past practice. You can simplify his job, assign him other work, put him on a special project, or ask him if he wants to retire early. Discuss these options with your superior before you offer any of them to Brian so that you do not make a commitment that you cannot carry out.

You seldom do people a favor when you continue to assign them jobs they cannot handle. Try to be helpful rather than critical. Ask, "How can we solve this problem?" Never say, "Your problem is. . . ." Get the person to suggest a solution or alternative and see if you can work it out that way.

When an employee has worked for an organization for many years, the company has an obligation to treat that worker fairly. Managers should be aware that their treatment of older workers will indicate to other employees how they can expect to be treated if their performance drops off.

How Another Supervisor Handled Poor Performance

Robert L., supervisor in a tire manufacturing plant in Union City, Tennessee, was aware that Ted N., one of his mechanics, had arthritis in his hands. Ted was in his early sixties and was very active, mentally and physically. Some of his fellow workers had suggested to him that he take a disability retirement, but Ted had emphatically turned that idea down, saying that he intended to work until he was at least 65 years old—and maybe even 70. But Robert could see that it was very painful for Ted to continue working with his hands and that his condition could not be expected to improve.

Fortunately, the tire company was implementing a training program for apprentice craftsmen and needed a trainer who understood the equipment and knew how to maintain and repair the various machines. With his experience and knowledge, Ted was an ideal candidate for the job. Robert recommended him for the position and Ted very quickly accepted when the company offered it.

In many firms where retirement-age people wish to continue

working, the company can profit from the individual's knowledge and experience—if someone recognizes those resources and sees that they are tapped. Supervisors, who have unique knowledge of each subordinate's capabilities and experience, can be very instrumental in finding the best position for an older person.

The older employee who has lost interest in the job

The Problem

Thelma P., reference librarian at the main library in a large city in Ohio, has worked in the library ever since her husband died ten years ago. When she started on the job at the age of 50, she was an enthusiastic person, still interested in broadening her education and welcoming the many requests that daily were made for her services. However, you, her supervisor, have noticed that Thelma seems to have lost interest in the job during the last year. She moves slowly now and sees little reason to pick up the tempo when helping people who come to her desk for information, even when a line begins to form. Thelma never arrives early in the morning and is the first person to leave in the evening. She refuses to work on Sundays during the winter months when the library is open in the afternoon. Her reason for not working these days is, "I've got a lot more important things to do on Sunday, such as visit my children and my grandchildren."

Since Thelma's lack of interest in the job has made her a handicap in serving the public, something should soon be done about her lack of performance on the job. But what?

The Solution

Change Thelma's responsibilities in the library to eliminate her contact with the public. Assign her planning and advisory duties, acquisitions and procurement responsibilities, filing and similar staff work. She can handle such tasks at her own pace. The benefits you may achieve with this move could be that Thelma may take a greater interest in the library's functions, become more loyal, and gain more satisfaction out of the job. You will, of course, have to assign a staff person to do the reference work, one who is much more efficient than Thelma.

It's probable that such an arrangement will suit everyone on your staff, since they have undoubtedly had more work to do and suffered occasional stress as a result of Thelma's lack of interest in the job. In the event that Thelma objects to your change in her responsibilities, you will have to explain that it is entirely normal for people to slow down on the job as they get older, but that the library is obliged to provide fast, efficient service for its patrons. Add that you are sure that she agrees with this.

As an alternative, suggest that Thelma take an early retirement. Her acceptance of this hinges on her financial status, her feelings of security, and her outside interests and hobbies. Remember that some employees do not plan for the day they retire and find it a very difficult time. Others have outside interests that are more important to them, such as a desire to travel or to be with their family.

How Another Supervisor Handled an Older Employee

Sarah G., supervisor of the test operators in an electrical appliance manufacturing firm in Iowa, noticed that one older employee, Ralph J., was not the friendly, enthusiastic worker that he had been several months ago. The man no longer seemed interested in his job, and he was noncommital and reserved with co-workers. In addition, Ralph had become unenthusiastic about accepting his assignments and seemed to carry a chip on his shoulder. He was quieter and more uncommunicative than he had ever been during the 15 years he had worked in the department.

Bothered by this behavior, Sarah decided to have a talk with Ralph. At first, Ralph was uncharacteristically embarrassed, but then he finally opened up. He revealed that he felt that Sarah was treating him like a man who was already over the hill; he claimed she gave him simple assignments that didn't use his talents and generally treated him condescendingly. Furthermore, Ralph felt he was not being seriously considered for the new supervisor's job that was opening up; with his record, experience, and training, he felt the job should be his. Instead, according to rumors, Ralph was being passed over in favor of a test operator who was much younger and had half his abilities.

In retrospect, Sarah had to admit that Ralph's conclusions could have been supported by their past communications, but she resolved to immediately set the record straight. She realized that, despite Ralph's age, he had many productive years left and wasn't ready to retire. In fact, from his record, he was the most likely person to be considered for the new supervisor's job. Sarah promptly assured Ralph that he rated high, in her opinion, on ability and experience, and that he was in the running for the new job. She apologized for having treated him condescendingly and promised it wouldn't happen again. Ralph again became his old self and did exceptional work in anticipation of being promoted.

This incident suggests two problems that all supervisors who have older people in their employ should be aware of. Although you may think that a senior worker's diminished performance or behavior is caused by a loss of interest in the job, you could be wrong. Do some talking and probing to find out the real reason. Also, be careful not to create problems when none exist, as Sarah did, by talking down to people and thereby insulting them.

The older employee who is no longer ambitious

The Problem

Hector C., veteran employee of your company in the accounting department, was very dejected when you spoke to him this morning.

At first he was reluctant to talk, but when you showed a sincere interest and said you were a good listener, he explained. Hector feels that he has achieved all his professional goals and that his salary is at its peak. He is worried about inflation and increasing family expenses. To add to his feeling of frustration, he believes that he has to stay in his present job, that he is too old to make a change or expect to find another job. He explained that he had "celebrated" his 59th birthday last month.

You may empathize with Hector's position and feeling, but what can you do or say to him that will change his outlook on life? You realize that his prospects for advancement are dim—the only position he could be promoted to is your job as supervisor, and you do not anticipate vacating that position in the near future.

The Solution

Talk to the personnel department of your company soon, asking that a search be made to find a new job for Hector. Being 59 years old should not be a deterrent to starting on a new job or career. If there is no current job opening that Hector could handle, ask that he be interviewed for the next one that opens up. But don't dismiss the problem at that point. Sit down with Hector to talk about his hobbies and his interests and ask him what type of work he would like to do. If he doesn't have an answer, tell him to think about it for a while and meet with you again. Plan a program of updating his knowledge and skills in his area of interest. Encourage him to read books and articles in that field and to take some courses at the local university. Hector needs to feel confident that he still has many years of productive contribution ahead. He should look for opportunities to use his store of knowledge and experience in new situations.

Let Hector know that you and the company value his experience. Add that he certainly knows his job better than you do and that you believe he could make valuable suggestions in other areas in the company. Ask him for his thoughts—he'll be flattered and you'll be helped. Older workers periodically need a boost to their egos, especially when they feel as Hector now does.

Although you may feel that your status as a supervisor is not likely to change, you should nevertheless train someone to be ready to take your place. Selecting Hector as your future replacement could give him a lift at a time when he sorely needs it.

How Another Supervisor Solved a Similar Problem

A few years ago Walter W. was a supervisor of a group of technicians in an electronic equipment manufacturing plant in New Jersey. The technicians were called upon to troubleshoot machine and equipment problems and make repairs. Because many of the control systems were solid-state and electronic, most of the people required special training. With one exception, the people in Walter's department were young. The exception was George B., a man who had 25 years of service with the company.

Walter first realized he had a problem when he noticed that George began to keep to himself in the work area and no longer volunteered for difficult jobs. Believing that George was feeling threatened by the younger technicians and that he had lost ambition because of it, Walter decided that he needed to restore George's enthusiasm and confidence. He did it by changing George's classification to "senior technician" and giving him an increase in pay. In addition, he told George to expect to be assigned many of the difficult jobs, ones where his knowledge and experience would enable him to diagnose equipment malfunctions faster than the younger technicians. Within a short time, George was his usual self again and the company was better off for it.

The older employee who shows hostility

The Problem

Hazel S., a woman who showed signs of resentment when you were named her supervisor, has worked in the billing office of the gas company for many years—in fact, she has been with the company for twenty years longer than you have. She has handled several different jobs, has generally mixed well with the other employees, and was usually friendly to everyone. But she has changed since the office was reorganized and two jobs were eliminated. Now Hazel doesn't join the group during the coffee-break period and doesn't say much except when someone tries to converse with her. What's worse, she has been so hostile when you've given her assignments that you fear she might refuse to do some job or do it poorly simply to cause you trouble. What's the problem with Hazel? How should you handle her? What should you say to reduce or eliminate the tension that has built up between you?

The Solution

The hostility of an older employee toward a young supervisor derives from several basic feelings. One, the most common, is fear. Hazel may be afraid that because of her age she is no longer a favored employee, that she could be discriminated against, and that she could lose her job. The severity of such feelings depends on how uncertain she is about her future with the company.

An older employee may also be jealous of and resent a younger person who has a higher position than his or hers, especially when the younger person is earning more money. Antagonism and withdrawal usually accompany such feelings.

Whatever the reason for Hazel's hostility, you must work to overcome it. Be friendly toward her and show that you respect her greater experience. Sincerity is very important in your relationship— you must continually demonstrate it. Although Hazel may have an unjustified contempt for you, you are responsible for resolving the difference. She is the offended person, the resentful one, and the one least likely to try to resolve the problem.

Don't forget that Hazel's ideals and goals may be quite different from yours. While she may be looking for security and awaiting her retirement, you may be concerned with your further advancement and status. Never hesitate to praise Hazel for work accomplished and jobs well done. This will not only tend to minimize her insecurity, but it will also boost her ego. The latter is very likely to bring an end to her hostility.

How Another Supervisor Handled Hostility

Everyone in the accounting department at the Baily Company in Illinois knew that either Pearl R. or Becky K. would be promoted when the next supervisory job opened up—and both the women sensed it too. An unexpressed yet obvious rivalry developed between them. Pearl, a woman in her fifties, possessed years of experience, but Becky, 30 years younger, had more formal education. Eventually, Becky got the job—to the dismay of Pearl.

Becky had anticipated the promotion and had planned how she would treat Pearl, who would be reporting to her. Becky expected Pearl to be hostile, but she decided not to do anything until the emotion was confirmed. When that happened, Becky immediately had a talk with Pearl. Becky told Pearl that she recognized Pearl's superior experience and wanted to learn from her. She asked for Pearl's help and cooperation, saying, "Knowing you, I really shouldn't have to ask for it, because I expect it." She assured Pearl that her status and responsibility on the job would remain the same, and that she ranked at the top of the list in capability and efficiency in the department. Although Pearl was uneasy when Becky began talking, she quickly accepted Becky's words and never displayed any hostility after that.

It may be only natural for an employee who is well educated to be arrogant and proud, but Becky never exhibited that "natural" tendency. As a result, she earned Pearl's trust and reduced any feelings of jealousy.

The older employee who has serious health problems

The Problem

Hugh F., senior electrician at the Motor Wheel plant in Lansing, Michigan, is 61 years old. He has 28 years of service with the company, the last 10 of which have been under your supervision. Early in his career he primarily did maintenance work. For the last few years he has been assigned new installations because of his extensive experience, his careful attention to detail, and his meticulous workmanship. He now has two junior electricians assisting him.

Hugh performs very well—when he's on the job. But he is a sick man who has had a variety of problems with his back and his kidneys. Attacks of arthritis have caused him to miss many days of work in the last year. Whenever he is absent, new installations progress much more slowly and the workmanship is often not up to standard.

Although you dislike facing up to the problem, you know that Hugh is too big a burden for your department to continue to support. What should be done? Should you suggest he be let go, despite his long years of service, or should you try to find some way to struggle along with him?

The Solution

This problem is difficult because you have a dual responsibility. On one hand, you must handle the workload with the company's best interests in mind—you can't permit new installations to be delayed or tolerate substandard work. But on the other hand, you have an obligation to a long-service employee with a good work record who has given so much of his life to the company.

The first thing you should do is talk to Hugh to see how he feels. Depending on your company's policy, he may be able to retire in a few years with a full pension. There's a possibility that he is staying on the job because he believes that doing otherwise would cause him to lose that pension. Try to reach some agreement with him. If he wants to take early retirement, perhaps in the near future you can find another job for him in the company for that period where his absences won't be critical. Find out what his reduced pension would be if he decides to retire now. He may be satisfied with that if he believes that his health is not going to improve. You might also talk to your superior about hiring him as a consultant after he retires. Do not suggest this to Hugh, however, until you are assured this arrangement could be made.

The last thing you should consider is recommending that he be let go. Twenty-eight years of loyal service deserves more humane consideration. You should be able to make some arrangement to keep him employed.

How Another Supervisor Handled a Health Problem

Rastus M., a laborer working for Clint W., supervisor of the janitorial group at the Mercy Hospital in Fayetteville, North Carolina, was in his sixties. He had always worked hard during his 22 years at the facility, despite the fact that most of his work was extremely demanding physically. When Rastus began to slow down on the job, Clint wondered if he should talk to him about retirement. Then one day he noticed that Rastus was suffering severe back pain. When he asked him about it, he learned that the laborer had developed a back problem a few months ago but had put off going to a doctor. Clint immediately insisted that Rastus be examined by one of the hospital's doctors to see what might be done for him. The doctor diagnosed the problem and recommended that Rastus take a sick leave, get his back put in traction, and follow this treatment with a change in job responsibilities to much lighter work. Rastus' back muscles had been overextended— he would never again be able to do any heavy lifting.

The treatment was begun the following week and successfully relieved his back pain. Rastus was back on the job three months later and resumed his laborer's duties at his former work pace, but only on tasks which didn't require lifting.

Older workers don't have the endurance they once had, and both mental and physical fatigue set in faster. Illnesses and accidents may keep older people off the job longer than they would younger workers, and invariably their bodies deteriorate to the point where physical capabilities are limited. But experience and skills often permit older people to compensate for these liabilities. Don't be in a hurry to write off senior workers when their health seems to be failing them. They may be able to give the company many more years of good performance.

8

The Employee with Personality Problems

Employees with personality problems are difficult to supervise. Their work habits, attitudes, and outlook on life are not always easy to understand, and those prone to public displays of emotion tend to reduce the morale and productivity of their work groups. For these reasons, supervisors cannot ignore employees who have personality problems, much as they might like to.

You cannot solve all personality problems, nor does management expect you to try to do so. Extreme cases, especially, must be left to psychiatrists and psychologists. But you can help some people by communicating with them, understanding them, and treating them the same way you treat other employees. You should be aware that people with personality problems are not easily changed and that disciplinary action is seldom effective.

The employee with personality problems who feels persecuted

The Problem

Nelda K. is a writer at the publishing company you work for in Barrington, Illinois. Your company publishes and sells posters, brochures, booklets, and a magazine for supervisors. Employers purchase your company's materials for bulletin boards and payroll inserts, and for use in training employees.

You rely on Nelda for much of the promotional material, ideas, and suggestions that provide the basis for the company's publications, especially those that come out monthly, such as the magazine. Nelda is very much aware of her responsibilities and feels the pressure to produce interesting and factual manuscripts. She is seldom at ease on the job. The infrequent letters criticizing the company's answers to human relations problems bother her, even though you and your superior edit and approve her work before it is published. Nelda also feels she is being persecuted whenever deadlines for the materials she writes are brought to her attention. You are concerned that these stresses may eventually cause her to leave the company. Is there anything you can say or do to alleviate Nelda's sense of persecution?

The Solution

Praising Nelda's efforts and her accomplishments will go a long way. An occasional complimentary word to her from your superior will also assure her that her work is appreciated and that she is not being harassed to do better.

There are other things you can say to Nelda to allay her feeling that she is being criticized for her answers to problems or for how long it takes her to produce them. Point out that everything she writes is edited by both you and your superior before it is published. If readers find fault with it, they are not finding fault with her but with the company. Explain how deadline dates are established and why they are necessary. Subscribers expect to receive the company's magazine the same time each month, and the publisher has an obligation to consistently deliver its product on time. Deadline information is also needed by the artists, copy writers, and editors to enable them to plan and schedule their work.

Whenever you communicate with Nelda, be sure to give her a chance to express her views and sentiments. She may feel that your communications are primarily in one direction—from you to her. Always make sure your instructions are clear and understood so that you will not have to repeat them, which might give her the impression that you are pushing her.

How Another Supervisor Handled a Similar Problem

Royal K., supervisor of the advertising group of a large department store in Los Angeles, realized that several people under his supervision were so sensitive to criticism that they felt persecuted almost every time he discussed their work with them. He was also aware that some of the other people could remain quite aloof when he commented on their work.

Royal decided that he could lessen feelings of persecution if he made his criticisms and suggestions of change in an impersonal manner. He was able to do this by devoting a part of his usual Friday afternoon meeting with his people to the subject. Without singling out an individual as guilty of an omission, poor approach, or mistake, he discussed such failings in general. With this "group therapy" action, Royal could caution his staff about pitfalls they should avoid in their work and not have anyone take such remarks as a personal admonishment. Royal knew that his department would see that he was treating each member the same and that they should not take his words personally.

In addition, Royal showed greater interest in the personal lives and problems of those employees who felt stress on the job. By indicating that he was concerned with their welfare, wanted them to get satisfaction from their work, and recognized the pressures that they frequently felt, he was able to greatly reduce their feelings of persecution.

The employee with personality problems who is easily hurt

The Problem

Your company, a large manufacturing firm with headquarters in Buffalo, New York, is in the midst of computerizing its stores' inventory and maintenance functions. You are a supervisor in the advanced systems department and have five programmers reporting to you. Management has placed a high priority on converting the stores' operations, and you were asked a month ago to put all your people on this task. Today, you learned that the project is not proceeding fast enough to suit the vice president. He has asked that you "whip your people into shape" by talking to each programmer individually and criticizing his or her slowness. This request puts you on the spot with one of your programmers, Norma W.

Norma is very sensitive to criticism and is easily hurt. Only a week ago she burst into tears when you questioned the scope of a program she had prepared for use by the supervisors in the maintenance department. She has recently been upset over remarks made by the male programmers about her work. What should you do about the request of the vice president with respect to Norma? How should you go about communicating with her in the future?

The Solution

There's no avoiding talking to Norma about making faster progress on the programming of the stores' functions, but you must use your best kid-gloves approach. Eliminate the personal factor as much as possible by frequent use of the words *we* and *our department* when talking about work and how it should be done.

At some point, every supervisor must tell subordinates to correct their errors and to upgrade their productivity. Be careful not to belittle people—that is hurtful. The more artfully you apply constructive criticism, the more effectively it will get the results you desire without causing stress. Because Norma is easily hurt, you must be especially careful when you communicate with her. Avoid saying anything that will undermine her self-confidence. Comment on and praise her work whenever you can.

Employees who are easily hurt by criticism must be continually assured that they are doing a good job. They also like to be thanked for their work. You must see that they do not misinterpret department decisions on job assignments if those assignments could reflect on their capabilities.

Unless people have deep-rooted problems, you will find that many of the expressed emotions can be dealt with if you are aware of what's behind them. For example, some employees object to their supervisors *telling* them to do something rather than *asking* them to do it. Others don't like to hear "*I* want it done this way." If you say *we* rather than *I,* the employee accepts it more willingly.

How Another Supervisor Meted Out Criticism

Helen B., supervisor in the mail department of an insurance company in New York, realized early in her career that supervisors need to be adept at criticizing employees without hurting their feelings. Along the way, she encountered one young fellow who presented a real challenge to her, until she recognized the basic problem.

Alex R., the son of one of the company's executives, was placed in the mail department as a first step in getting experience. Alex was intelligent and ambitious, and within a month of starting work he had come up with an idea to speed up operations in the department. The recognition he received augmented his already egotistical attitude, and he became a bit obnoxious. Helen decided that Alex's ego could stand to be deflated, so she began to criticize him for one thing or another. Although this treatment subdued him considerably, something Helen hadn't bargained for also happened. He began to be unsure of himself, hesitant, and reluctant to make suggestions. It finally dawned on Helen that Alex's bravado was his way of compensating for an underlying sense of inadequacy, despite his talent and skills. She had a talk with him in which she let him know that she held him in very high regard. But she commented that showing off produces resentment and hostility in other employees. He got the message and went on to higher positions in the company.

The employee with personality problems who is frequently angry

The Problem

Richie J., an instrument mechanic in the maintenance department of a chemicals plant in New Jersey, seemed well qualified and suited for the job when he was hired several months ago, but he turned out to be hard to get along with. He becomes angry at the slightest provocation, and sometimes shows his anger with alarming and disturbing behavior. At first, his anger was taken out on the operators of the instruments he was assigned to repair. Several times he directly accused them of deliberately damaging the controls in order to make work for him. On one occasion he threw a bottle of ink against the wall in the control room.

For several weeks, most of Richie's temper tantrums were considered harmless, but lately his behavior has become disruptive. Last week he insisted on bothering the plant manager, claiming that someone had stolen one of his tools and that if it wasn't returned, he would take a tool from one of the other mechanics. He also became quite angry when the plant manager refused to take action personally, but instead referred Richie to you, his supervisor. How should you handle him? Would disciplinary measures be appropriate?

The Solution

Richie must be told that in view of his behavior, management is entitled to know if he's in a fit condition to continue working for the company. He should be informed that his inability to control his temper is disruptive and abusive. It's management's right to request that he see a psychiatrist who would report the results of his examination to the company. Preferably, you should ask the company doctor to talk to him and tell him about this management decision.

You can expect that Richie will become very angry with the company's request that he be examined. Be prepared to insist and to say that if he persists in refusing the examination, it will cost him his job. You should certainly not attempt to diagnose the behavior or try to correct it alone.

People who frequently "fly off the handle" and are constantly angry are emotionally immature. They may also have a strong inferiority complex. Disciplinary action may not succeed in correcting displays of temper and irrational behavior, but it may persuade the individual that the company will not tolerate such behavior. Let the employee know that if the problem is not corrected, the individual may lose his or her job.

How Another Supervisor Handled Anger

Roger P., a supervisor in a steel mill in Youngstown, Ohio, learned that the best way to get along with a person who is frequently angry is to step up communications with the person as much as possible, particularly when you are sure you can control your own emotions. He took this approach when he was conducting his annual interviews with each of his shop leaders. Just a few hours before the interview, Arthur had been accused of discriminating against a minority employee by one of the union leaders, a subject that Roger planned to discuss with him.

Arthur had always treated minorities fairly and was proud of it. When Roger brought the subject up, Arthur became so angry that Roger tactfully suggested that they postpone the interview. At the same time, he assured Arthur that he understood his feelings. Roger followed up by showing an interest in Arthur and by expressing a desire and willingness to sit down and talk another time. They soon did, and the interview went off well.

Talking constructively with an angry person is difficult, if not impossible. If a person becomes emotional, you must listen, not talk. An angry person is expressing a mixture of feelings that may include resentment, frustration, fear, prejudice, and disappointment. The person may not mention these feelings, but you will be aware of them if you listen carefully.

Don't try to persuade an angry person to change, and don't suggest that both of you talk about something else. When a person is angry or otherwise emotional, his or her mind cannot be turned to another subject.

The employee with personality problems who talks too much

The Problem

Connie M., a veteran employee in the office services group that you supervise, is capable of doing the work you assign her. However, she is the kind of worker who must be kept under constant supervision. Connie's problem is her seemingly endless chatter during working hours. She frequently leaves her desk to gab with someone in another department, and some of her conversations are conducted on the office phone. You've talked to her twice about monopolizing the office phone and making it difficult for work-related calls to get through. Your suggestions that she minimize personal calls have been ignored.

When you went to her desk today to give her special instructions about a high-priority job, she was talking on the phone. You waited patiently for a few minutes, then left when you could see that the conversation was going to continue. When you returned 15 minutes later, she was still talking. This time you interrupted, telling her to break it off and see you as soon as possible. She was quite indignant and wanted to know why you were making a big fuss. She claimed that company policy allowed employees to receive and make personal phone calls, that everyone else makes them, and that she shouldn't be singled out for criticism.

What should you do about Connie's repeated gabbing and her apparent refusal to change her ways? Should you suggest to your boss that she be fired?

The Solution

The employee who wastes time talking too much is not only failing to be productive but is also wasting the time of others. Point this out to Connie. Tell her that you have had to guard against the practice of talking too much yourself and that many people on the job have the same problem. This softens your criticism. Explain that a long conversation takes up valuable time of the person making the call as well as the person listening. A person must be considerate of others who may not have the time to spend chatting but are too polite to say anything about it.

You may be able to have Connie fired eventually, but not until you can build up a documented case against her. Even though you may have talked to her repeatedly about her abuse of telephone privileges and her excessive gabbing on the job, that's not enough to get her fired. Check with your personnel department to see if there have been other situations in which disciplinary action was taken because of excessive talking. It could provide guidance for how to handle Connie.

To build your case against Connie and also to get her to reform so that you don't have to mete out discipline, send her an official written notice recounting today's incident. Be sure that a copy of the letter goes in her file in the personnel department. If that doesn't curb her talkativeness, give her some time off without pay, and warn her that the next offense will be dealt with more harshly. Follow through until you get compliance or have enough evidence to recommend that she be fired.

If an employee persists in wasting his or her time and that of other employees with excessive bull sessions or idle gossip, a supervisor must take action. Nonproductive employees are an expense that no company can afford.

How a Supervisor Handled Excessive Talking in Meetings

Maxwell R., supervisor at the Thompson Company in Chicago, held biweekly department meetings to update research and development projects and to discuss current company problems. Maxwell actively solicited opinions and comments from participants in order to ensure that subjects were covered from all possible viewpoints and that no alternative answer to a problem was overlooked. But he had a problem accomplishing this objective: one of the members of the group, Gary R., was an extroverted and egotistical person who frequently dominated the discussion, and other people had trouble joining in.

At first, Maxwell ignored Gary and hoped that he would get the message that Maxwell preferred to hear from the others. When this didn't work, he talked to Gary after a meeting. Maxwell told him that he recognized Gary's superior analytic abilities. When these words inflated Gary's ego, Maxwell immediately followed up by asking Gary to withhold his opinions and comments during meetings until all the others had had a chance to talk. The next meeting went much better.

Controlling a person who talks too much may require aggressive action on your part, but instead of bluntly telling the person to shut up, you can get the message across in other ways. You might, for example, force someone like Gary to justify a statement or an idea, particularly if it is farfetched. After one or two embarrassing situations, the talker will begin to think twice before speaking.

The person who talks too much in meetings may not be as serious a problem as you think. You must recognize that a loquacious person can keep a discussion active and moving. If other people in a meeting are reticent and reluctant to speak up, he or she may be the catalyst to draw them out, so you may not wish to suppress such a person completely.

The employee with personality problems who is eccentric and unpredictable

The Problem

Mike, an advertising copywriter, is a talented and creative person. He's young and single, and his offbeat personality and style are manifested in unconventional work habits. Although Mike gets his work done and often does it in an innovative and ingenious manner, he is late to work more often than any other of the people you supervise, and takes many days off for "personal reasons." This habit is especially irritating to you when he is working on what you consider an urgent project.

Copywriters sometimes work closely with clients in your company. You are not pleased with how Mike comes across in such situations. While other copywriters generally follow accepted dress and behavior codes, Mike's appearance and demeanor vary radically and seem to depend on his mood, which changes from day to day. He might come to work wearing a sports jacket and slacks or he could show up in a sweater and worn jeans. In addition, his carefree manner in dealing with clients makes you wonder if he gives them a false impression of the agency's reputation, accomplishment, and desire to perform a high-quality service.

Should you continue to accept Mike's eccentric and unpredictable behavior? Is there anything you can do to change it? Should you recommend that the company get rid of him?

The Solution

It is unlikely that you or anybody else can change Mike's lifestyle or the way he handles his job. His background, upbringing, and attitude have coalesced and he is apparently satisfied with himself and the work he does. This is confirmed by his carefree demeanor. You can see and judge Mike in one of two ways, depending on whether you let your emotions rule or whether you try to be practical. If he were a production or maintenance employee, his style and the manner in which he works would be unacceptable. But he is a professional whose work habits have little effect on the quality or quantity of work he turns out, and clients apparently have accepted that or you would have been told otherwise.

A different set of behavior rules may be said to apply to highly creative people like Mike. Such people often have big egos, are independent, and are difficult to control. They require special handling, but the company should not get rid of them, especially if they continue to contribute.

Creative people want and expect personal freedom. They should be given latitude to pursue and develop new ideas. The creative urge they possess is stimulated by challenge and inhibited by routine. They thrive on intricate problems that only their intelligence and talents can handle. Most are very competent and take pride in their accomplishments.

You will always find it difficult to decide if an eccentric person's behavior is harmful or a serious matter for other reasons. Most of the time you should simply recognize what you are facing and make the best of it. Surprisingly, once you try to go along with the behavior, you will usually decide that you really don't have a problem after all.

How Another Supervisor Dealt with Eccentric Behavior

Dom D. is a supervisor in a plastics job shop in Detroit. His company fabricates various plastic structures and models to order, and also cuts and assembles bulk orders of rods, blocks, and sheets for consumers. Employees are encouraged to design and construct knickknacks and toys that the company markets.

One of Dom's subordinates, Ralph, was quite eccentric, although extremely creative. He delighted in coming up with bizarre figures, unusual formations, and unrealistic fabrications. Although Ralph's design attempts often wasted time and material, they did provide the company with many marketable pieces of art. However, the gyrations and antics that Ralph went through in creating his "masterpieces" disrupted the efforts of other employees.

Dom realized that if he were to give his prima donna special treatment he would arouse resentment in other employees. This could result in a letdown on the job as well as a loss of respect for him as a supervisor. Yet he did not want to suppress Ralph's creativity. Dom resolved the problem by treating Ralph the same as he treated all other employees; he showed neither favor nor disfavor with his behavior. However, he never let his prima donna get by on nerve alone. He would challenge Ralph occasionally on his choice of subjects on which to spend time.

A supervisor's favored treatment of an eccentric employee suggests to others the wrong performance criteria for doing a good job. Instead of reinforcing the fact that outstanding work is most important, the supervisor is indicating that the person who puts on the best performance is most accepted.

The employee with personality problems who is negative and pessimistic

The Problem

Alex M. has been working in the job shop under your supervision for more than three years; previously, he had been a production-line employee. Your company in Detroit, Michigan, manufactures a wide range of plastic products and conducts a considerable amount of development and test work to assure that the products are useful, will sell readily in the marketplace, and are designed with convenience as well as safety in mind. Much of the work in the job shop consists in determining why a product failed in service, testing new designs, and making value analysis studies in order to reduce costs.

Although Alex is skilled with his hands, he is a pessimist who frequently thinks of reasons why goals can't be reached, why ideas won't work, and why something new or different doesn't stand a chance. He believes that things should be left as they are. Thus, it is difficult for you to get Alex enthusiastic about his work. Also, you are never sure if he has really tried to correct a deficiency or malfunction when he gives up on it. You don't want to pair him with another worker on jobs for fear that his gloomy attitude will influence the other worker's thinking. Is there anything you can do to get Alex to think more positively?

The Solution

The next time Alex comes to you with a negative response, shake him up by demanding that he come up with some positive alternatives. If he says something won't work, give him the job of discovering what will. You may have to go through a period of seemingly low productivity from Alex when you do this, but you'll be jolting him out of his rut. You will also help him respect those people who do make constructive suggestions on the job.

Becoming optimistic will not be easy for Alex. You cannot expect a complete switch on his part, because his negativism is probably deeply ingrained. But those changes you do bring about will make him a more cooperative person. Be sure you are always positive when communicating with him. Indicate that you are optimistic when you discuss a tough problem that you have assigned him. If he has respect for you, your attitude is bound to make an impression on him.

The secret of getting people to think positively is to convince them that such thinking is best for them. Tell Alex that he will enjoy his work more and get more satisfaction from it if he gets more involved with it. Say that optimism leads to a drive that causes things to work out better. Very likely he will be skeptical about your assertions, but you must persuade him to give the theory a try.

To help demonstrate the value of positive thinking, remind Alex about the feats of people who wouldn't accept failure and whose perseverance led to breakthroughs in technology, medicine, and business. The electric light bulb and heart transplants became possible because someone believed they were possible and worked hard to prove it.

How Another Supervisor Accentuated the Positive

Amanda P., supervisor of the stockkeepers in a catalog supply house in Georgia, thought that she was going to have to recommend to management that Roy G. be fired. Roy had worked as a bartender in a local night club, a truck driver, and a gas station attendant before coming to the supply house. He had never been able to hold a job for any length of time and had developed a negative attitude about work in general. This attitude was reflected in the way he handled his job as stockkeeper. Roy was careless in his work habits, loafed, and frequently made mistakes in filling orders. When complaint letters from customers brought such errors to the attention of management, Amanda was told to either straighten Roy out or get rid of him.

Amanda was a strong advocate of accentuating the positive and believed that praising a worker will not spoil him. She always looked for a little good in the worst worker and praised him or her for it. Faced with Roy's poor performance and knowing that she would have to get him to improve or else recommend that he be fired, Amanda embarked on a praise-and-compliment course with him. She began by mentioning that she had noticed that Roy had not missed a day of work for some time, and went on to say that she appreciated having a stockkeeper she could depend on. She started singling out orders that she knew Roy could handle without difficulty and then praised him for doing a good job. And when Roy took a minimum number of breaks during the day, Amanda complimented him with such remarks as, "Thanks, Roy, you really put out today." It wasn't long before Roy did a much better job every day.

When supervisors convey a positive attitude to their workers, the workers feel good and want to do a better job. But it goes beyond that. Workers who see their job as a positive part of their life *because the boss is sincere and sees the good in their performance* will be more satisfied with their work and will actually *do a better job.*

9

The Other Supervisor

Getting along well with your fellow supervisors makes your job more pleasant and enjoyable. Management likes to see compatibility and cooperation among supervisory people because that makes it easier for the company to attain its goals and objectives. Unfortunately, supervisory people in competitive positions occasionally differ in the way they view their duties and responsibilities on the job. To resolve differences, supervisors must understand each other and must *want* to get along with each other.

You must recognize that other supervisors have goals to meet and commitments to honor. They have problems, just as you do, and each one feels that he or she knows how those problems can best be solved. Always consider how your actions affect the operation of other departments. Make decisions that will help rather than hinder them. Most problems of getting along with another supervisor can be solved by communicating with him or her. By talking about your differences and bringing to light how cooperation can solve them, both you and the other supervisor will benefit.

The other supervisor who
goes to your boss to discuss your differences

The Problem

Kate R., supervisor of the sewers in the women's apparel company where you work, was promoted to the job from the group she now supervises. You, supervisor of the cutters and trimmers, came to the company from the company's major competitor. Both of you must closely coordinate your efforts in order to meet the company's production schedule, which is no easy task when you must deal with shortages of material, equipment downtime, and absenteeism.

Recently, you've had another problem to contend with. One of Kate's sewers told you privately the other day that Kate had been telling your and Kate's supervisor that you were doing a poor job of managing your department, and were making her job more difficult. Kate blamed your poor performance on your tendency to follow your former company's practices, which resulted in lost time on the job. Kate has never mentioned this to you but you have noticed that lately she has not gone out of her way to be friendly. What should you do? Should you confront her with what you heard? Should you bring up the subject with your supervisor?

The Solution

Poor communication on the job occurs most often not between bosses and subordinates, but among department supervisors who must work together. Other supervisors can do more to impede your progress or turn cold water on your ideas than anyone else.

Confronting Kate with what you heard is not recommended. It would immediately put her on the defensive and would not improve your relationship. A better way to handle the problem is to adopt a plan of working more closely with her on your mutual problems. Start communicating with Kate by saying words such as, "Everyone knows you are capable and conscientious and have years of experience to guide you on the job. But our departments, yours and mine, must operate in an organized way. You and I must work together as a team—we must be aware of what each other's problems are and adjust our own work accordingly. I know you'll want to cooperate with me, won't you?" Not only do such words explain how things are, they also let Kate know you expect her to go along with you.

You have to sell yourself to Kate. If you are accepted, then it will be easier for her to incorporate your ideas. Selling yourself may take a long time, but don't give up. Try to meet with her daily. Review your problems and your plans. Ask for her opinions. For some reason, Kate resents some of your ideas, either because she hasn't come up with them herself or because she feels you are getting ahead of her. A way to contend with peer rivalry is to be very open with her about your thoughts and ideas. You can even imply that you picked up some of the ideas from other supervisors. Another way is to present a problem to her and lead her into suggesting the solution. Her ego will receive a boost when you accept her answer to the problem.

You have nothing to gain by talking with your superior about Kate. If your superior considered it a problem, you would have heard about it. It's also better that you don't get involved in trying to defend yourself when you have done nothing wrong—don't give the impression that you are concerned with petty matters.

The impression you make on other supervisors affects their and your ability to get a job done. No matter how intelligent you are or how self-perceptive you may be, you simply cannot see yourself the way other people see you. That's why it's so important that you communicate and get feedback from the people you must work with as a team. The supervisor who always compliments other supervisors finds it easy to get along with them. You're much better off if you avoid criticizing them; you won't get ahead on the job by tearing someone else down.

How Another Supervisor Resolved a Similar Problem

When Roger W., supervisor of the mechanics in a tool manufacturing plant in Lansing, Michigan, heard that a peer had been discussing with their superior how Roger handled his department, he immediately decided to find out if what he was doing was wrong and if his subordinates resented his method of supervising. Fortunately, he had a longtime friend at a higher-level job in another department of the company. After he had explained the situation to him, the friend agreed to talk to some people to find out what they thought of Roger as a supervisor. The friend learned that Rogers was looked upon as more of a driver than a leader and his people resented his habit of constant checking on them as they did their work. Thanking his friend for his help, Roger began a self-improvement program. Soon he was respected as a supervisor and more liked by his people.

The other supervisor who doesn't enforce the rules

The Problem

The company you work for believes that order and control by management is possible only if work rules are clearly defined and enforced. Generally, the employees recognize this and accept it, particularly when the rules affect their health and safety. A few years ago the company was fined by a government agency for violating two safety rules. Since that time, you have been very careful and insist that your people follow all the work rules in your department.

But there are always a few employees who will not abide by the rules. Several of them work in the department next to yours under the supervision of Jack C. Jack is an extroverted, carefree person; he enjoys practical jokes both on and off the job. A lackadaisical person, he gives the impression that he's a member of the production crew rather than its supervisor—and this demeanor is reflected in his style of supervision. He doesn't attempt to enforce rules, with the result that your people often complain, "Why should we have to do that? They don't do it in Jack's department." You have no problem when rules concerning health and safety are involved because you can easily justify and answer them. But rules on beginning and quitting work, break and lunch times, and horseplay are another matter. How should you handle Jack's failure to enforce these rules? How do you answer the people in your department?

The Solution

A supervisor who is tough, fair, and knows the job is one who is most effective. Such a leader is also respected.

Stick by your guns when it comes to enforcing the rules, but always explain why those rules are made and why they must be followed. You know that Jack is doing a poor job of supervising when he doesn't enforce the rules, and your subordinates know it too. Some of the people who are complaining are really testing you to see if you will bend. Others may be out to get all they can—it's your job to keep them in line.

Don't think that management isn't aware of your problems. Laxness in rule enforcement shows up in performance on the job. A department supervised by a manager who does not exercise control exhibits poorer safety records, lower productivity, and weaker morale. Housekeeping is sloppy and absenteeism high. When management decides to do something about such conditions, a change in supervision is the first step.

At an opportune time, tactfully tell Jack about the comments of your people. Ask him for help; don't complain. Although Jack's initial response may be to joke about it, your words may cause him to think twice when he sees a rule ignored by one of his people. Always avoid acting indifferent and disinterested when working on problems that other supervisors could and should solve. Keeping the communication channels open until the problem is solved often takes patience, persistence, and tact.

Some supervisors don't believe in enforcing trivial rules. Unfortunately, a lax attitude often causes problems. Work rules are sometimes hard to understand, but they seldom pertain to just one department. A rule that seems minor in one operation may be major in another, although a supervisor may lack the overview to understand that fact.

How Another Supervisor Handled a Similar Problem

Willard C., supervisor in the fiber processing department of a container manufacturing plant near Chicago felt that he needed the cooperation of Ralph K., supervisor in the pulp processing department, in order to enforce work procedures and rules. Willard's and Ralph's departments both supplied the mixing and compounding department. Willard, much more experienced than Ralph in handling people on the job, saw that he could not ignore Ralph's weakness in enforcing the rules if he were to prevent friction between his and Ralph's people. Therefore, he worked out ways to improve communication and promote teamwork between the two departments.

Willard treated Ralph as a partner rather than an opponent. He offered to help Ralph whenever he had an opportunity, and he compromised on differences in order to achieve compatibility. Whenever he asked Ralph to do something for him, he explained the reasons for the request and pointed out the benefits to Ralph of going along. Willard understood the difference between cooperation and interference—he always dealt with Ralph rather than with Ralph's subordinates when he wanted help. Within a short period of time, Ralph and Willard saw eye to eye on the necessity of enforcing the rules relating to the work and performance of their people.

Any supervisor who attempts to handle responsibilities without working with other supervisors is likely to get in trouble. Teamwork is necessary to solve today's work and personnel problems and maintain productivity. Effective teamwork requires good communication among supervisors and a willingness to cooperate in working toward goals.

The other supervisor who takes credit for your work

The Problem

Oscar H. is the production supervisor on the shift before yours in the paint manufacturing company in El Paso, Texas, where you both work. The plant operates three shifts because of the volume of the company's business and the fact that some of the process reactions run 12 hours. Since many of the batch operations proceed simultaneously, good records must be kept of each process, including records of the segregation of various products. Much of the information is kept on process sheets located near the equipment; problems, answers, and miscellaneous information is written in a logbook kept in the factory's office.

Oscar is very egotistic and ambitious. Although he's basically honest, he will take credit for as much work as he can, and this is where you have a problem. Many times he takes credit for a job completed by your shift. Also, he occasionally forgets to pass instructions and special handling procedures on to you, with the result that a particular job either doesn't get done or is done incorrectly. These omissions make you look bad to your superior, and the work Oscar takes credit for makes it appear that he accomplishes more than you. What should you do about Oscar?

The Solution

Be very careful that *your* records, notes, answers to problems, and reports of events are clear and complete. Provide pertinent remarks about specific accomplishments to show that your department, rather than Oscar's, actually did the work. When you become known for factual reporting, there will never be any doubt as to which shift did the work.

The way for you to get truthful reporting from Oscar is to personally check plant conditions before he leaves. Come to work early enough to see for yourself the state of the various operations and to read the logbook. Follow up with casual statements about his reports. If he passes such observations off lightly, make a point of handing him the log or record and saying, "Here, you'll want to change this." You shouldn't have to do this very often for him to get the message.

To handle the problem of forgotten instructions, ask your boss to put these instructions in writing, either in the logbook or in a memo to you.

To check on this, get in the habit of asking Oscar before he leaves, "Is there anything I should watch out for?"

Almost all incidents of another supervisor taking credit for something you did will be unintentional. You should always treat them as such. Nothing can destroy good relations with your peers as much as false or unjust accusations, so it's better to say nothing rather than risk that possibility.

Mistakes and the inability to handle jobs are sometimes due to lack of cooperation among supervisors. The situation can be critical when the company operates with two or more shifts. Don't assume that other supervisors know something about a job or work in progress simply because you know about it—ask them if they're aware of what you know. If you must report on a plant or office problem to a supervisor on the next shift, use some record forms or a department logbook.

How Another Supervisor Made Sure That Credit Was Properly Given

Whenever Horace W., supervisor in the production department in an insulation supply company in Illinois, suspected that another person was being given credit for something he did, he made sure to mention something specific about the job when talking with his superior. By discussing the time it took to do the job or the number of people who participated, he was able to convey the extent of his department's involvement in the task. But that wasn't all he accomplished in such discussions. He "blew his own horn" a bit and made management aware of his interest, enthusiasm, and capabilities. He also justified his position with the company and paved the way for his eventual promotion.

Smart supervisors make sure that their superiors are periodically updated on their abilities and accomplishments, especially when they are working off-shifts and see their superiors infrequently or for short periods of time. There's nothing wrong with this if you do it discretely and tactfully.

The other supervisor who tries to pass responsibilities on to you

The Problem

You and Clara B. are supervisors of the sales clerks in a large department store in Chicago. Clara's responsibilities include women's wear, household items, jewelry, cosmetics, and appliances, among others. You handle men's wear, furniture, hardware, automotive, sporting goods, and so on. In addition to supervising the clerks, both of you work closely with buyers and advertising people. You report requests for items, take and report inventories, and suggest price reductions and features for sales promotions. Clara has tried to pass some of her inventory responsibilities onto you. For example, since the men's shoes and women's shoes are side by side and are procured through one buyer, Clara asked you to work with the buyer in ordering women's shoes, saying, "I'm very poor at predicting sales and deciding what should be ordered." Caught off-guard, you agreed to do it. That happened shortly after she became supervisor a few months ago. Today, Clara came to you asking if you would also work with the buyers of jewelry. This time, you told her you would think about it and get back to her later. What should you do about this supervisor who is trying to shirk her responsibilities?

The Solution

When you get back to Clara, explain that what she has asked you to do is *her* responsibility, one that you are not prepared to take. Explain that doing this job for her can only lead to problems for both of you. Also tell her that you've referred the shoe buyer back to Clara for information on buying women's shoes because you were handling that aspect of Clara's job only until she became more experienced.

Another way to answer Clara's new request is to simply say to her, "I'm sure you can handle this once you know the procedure. Why don't I work on it with you once or twice until you catch on? Of course, you will have to make the final decisions." Clara will have no recourse but to accept your offer.

To avoid situations like this, you must be careful about what you say when it is apparent that a peer is trying to escape the burden of a problem. The best response isn't "How can we solve this problem?" It is instead, "When we finish talking about this problem, which of us is going to carry the load of worrying about it?"

Solving problems for peers can stifle their growth and it can diminish your effectiveness. The supervisor who makes too many such agreements will find less and less time and energy available for his or her own duties.

How Another Supervisor Handled the Problem of Job Responsibility

Bob M., an experienced supervisor in a paper mill in Wisconsin, was accustomed to working with new supervisors, some of whom were quite concerned with the responsibilities of their job and asked for his help. The company frequently assigned new supervisors to operations closely related to his because it was a good area for training them. Bob was often asked to help a new man on the job and willingly did so. Very seldom was he asked to take on some of the responsibilities of the new supervisor, yet he had an answer for those occasions. He replied by saying, "Sure, I'll be glad to do that for you, but we'll have to clear it with the boss. You know, management has studied all these jobs and written up detailed descriptions of them. They would like to know if we transfer a responsibility to another position." Invariably, the new supervisor changed his mind and did the job to the best of his or her ability.

10

The Unreasonable Boss

During your career, you'll probably work for several bosses, one or more of whom you'll feel is unreasonable. You'll find, however, that the successes of such people become your successes. Unreasonable as a boss can be, you can usually further your career by going along with him or her.

Being in charge means exercising authority and giving orders, and those responsibilities don't enhance a person's popularity. But the more ineffectual and the less demanding you permit your boss to be with you, the weaker you'll be as a leader of your own department. Conversely, working for a boss who is hard to please and who gives you too much work provides good training in how to handle similar problems with your own subordinates. If your boss won't listen or is always too busy to see you, you'll learn not to be that way yourself.

This is not to say that you should always accept an unreasonable boss. Let your feelings be known to him or her. Most bosses will take time to discuss such matters. And, more often than you might think, they will change their ways to have better relations with you. Sometimes it is only necessary to bring their attention to the problem.

The unreasonable boss who gives you too much work

The Problem

You have been the supervisor of the finishing and inspection departments in an aluminum products plant in West Bend, Wisconsin, for five years. Twenty people report to you. The company has done well in the last few years and is growing. Last month, six new products were added to the company's line, bringing the total to 30. But quality-control problems have arisen with the new products. Today, your boss gave you the job of finding out what is wrong and recommending corrective action.

While you welcome the challenge and view it as an opportunity to show what you can do, you feel that you don't have the time to work on the problem. The boss assigned four additional people to your department a month ago when the new products came out—and you felt that you were already overworked supervising 16 people. What should you do about the additional work you are being asked to do?

The Solution

Many bosses have a very unclear view of all that their subordinates do or are capable of doing. So they simply add responsibilities if they think the subordinates can handle them. In your case, the boss apparently thinks highly of you or he would not have asked you to solve the quality-control problem. Part of his tendency to pile more work on you may be due to his awareness of the limitations of some of his other supervisors.

Accept the new assignment and consider it as a temporary problem. You can probably solve it quickly, faster than you now think. After you do, you will have two good reasons for going after an increase in your pay: (1) the increased number of people you now supervise and (2) your achievement on the quality-control problem.

Many supervisors are overworked because they don't have the nerve to tell their bosses when they're overloaded. There's always the possibility that the boss doesn't know *all* of what you've got to do. Don't be afraid to admit it when you simply haven't the time to take on that extra assignment. After all, your supervisor doesn't want you to do an inadequate job on something important.

You must be careful, however, when talking about your workload. It is tempting to describe how much you're doing and point out how little another supervisor is responsible for. Unfortunately, that may merely cause the boss to defend the other supervisor's workload without changing yours. Besides, stating or implying that something is unfair is not likely to change the boss's mind. He or she has probably already thought about what's fair, just as you do when assigning work to your people.

A subtle way to handle a boss who gives you too much work is to ask, "Which of my present assignments should I drop in order to handle this new one?"

How Another Supervisor Reacted to an Additional Assignment

Tony R., supervisor of the melt, pour, and strip workers at a foundry in Gary, Indiana, was constantly on the move in the large facility the company operated. Since the product line varied from week to week, there never seemed to be an end to the problems his people encountered with the molds and the castings. He was therefore surprised when his boss suggested to him one day that he also supervise the touch-up crew. Tony sat down with his boss and simply laid out the evidence—he showed how he was already up to his neck in work. He explained that the new responsibility would increase his load by as much as 20 percent. He admitted he couldn't manage to maintain his usual thoroughness in seeing that the castings met specifications and were of high quality if his workload was increased.

Tony's boss took another look at the responsibilities of all his supervisors and agreed that Tony was right. Supervision of the touch-up crew was assigned to another supervisor.

The unreasonable boss who is hard to please

The Problem

Mr. Thompson, your boss, heads the company you work for, an art supply and paper products firm in Philadelphia. You are the supervisor of the clerks and you also assist in the purchasing function. While you like your work, your job would be more pleasant and enjoyable if your boss weren't so hard to please.

Mr. Thompson is a perfectionist and a hard worker. He didn't start his own company until late in life after he'd become very experienced in business operations. But, in your opinion, he manages the company more closely than necessary. For example, he gets involved with details that he should leave to others. He doesn't accept performance of a task unless he feels that it was the best the employee was capable of doing. And he has definite preferences, which he clearly expresses, on many matters. He continually tells you how he would have done something or describes what you should have done. Can you do anything to improve your relations with Mr. Thompson? Would you be better off to look for another job?

The Solution

Several things can happen when you regard your boss as unapproachable or hard to please. You may develop a rebellious state of mind, stifle suggestions you would otherwise offer, limit your cooperation, and even gloat over things that go wrong. All of these attitudes and actions hurt the company *and* you, although you may not realize it. You might be better off if you would simply accept your boss "as is." Otherwise, you'll only increase your feeling of incompatibility.

You cannot change Mr. Thompson, nor should you expect that anyone else will. He has been hard to please for a long time and will continue to be that way. It's his nature. If you can't live with it, start looking for another job. But be aware that your next boss may also be that way.

Bosses are not always likable people, and some are difficult to work for. But when you are employed by someone, you should really work for that person. You were hired as a supervisor. If you don't do a good job of supervising, you're failing the boss *and* the company.

Bosses are human. Few of them are hard to please simply for the sake of being difficult. Most bosses are dedicated and have a deep sense of responsibility toward their work. They enjoy getting projects started and seeing positive results. They demand careful work and a thorough investigation of problems—they dislike hasty, off-the-cuff answers. Successful bosses are not clock watchers, and they expect their people to be the same. They hate to leave a job incomplete.

You may think your supervisor is hard to please if he or she is critical of others. But most bosses worry about people who are not doing their best work. They sincerely want everybody to succeed.

How Another Supervisor Handled a Hard-to-Please Boss

Mary A., newly promoted supervisor of the order clerks in a catalog house in Houston, Texas, felt at first that she had a demanding boss. But as she got to know her superior better, she realized she was mistaken. Mary saw that if she was going to get along well with her boss, she would have to see Eleanor as a unique individual and not as a stereotype. With this in mind, Mary decided to learn about her boss's strengths and weaknesses, her work habits, and her outlook on life. She also looked for clues that indicated when her boss was upset, was under pressure, and needed help.

In the process of getting to know her boss better, Mary learned that when she went out of her way to support Eleanor, she was much easier to please. In addition, Eleanor was very appreciative of Mary's efforts to keep her informed. One of the serious deterrents to good boss–subordinate relations is the tendency of the subordinate to modify reports to make them seem favorable, to present half-truths, or to conveniently forget to mention something that went wrong. Supervisors may think that they are shielding the boss from problems that might prove disturbing, but in the long run the practice of hiding unpleasant experiences from the boss is harmful to him or her and to the company. Mary was, therefore, completely frank and honest with her boss at all times. This, perhaps more than anything else, made Eleanor seem much easier to please.

The unreasonable boss who doesn't listen

The Problem

Although you feel you're doing a good job as supervisor of the telephone operators and receptionists at the central offices of a bank in New York, you know that your job would be easier if your boss would listen more often and carefully to what you tell her. Last week, for example, you told Margaret W., your boss, that one of the workers was taking a leave of absence during the holiday season and that Margaret should arrange for temporary help. Margaret did not make the arrangements. Two days ago you asked for a day of vacation and she granted it, but today she asked you why you weren't on the job yesterday. A more serious matter was her not listening when she was preparing the department budget—you told her that the operators would need new chairs this year and to include that item as a department expense. The item was not in the budget, and when you put through a change Margaret was criticized by management.

What is the problem with Margaret? Is there anything you can do to get her to be a better listener?

The Solution

When supervisors complain that their bosses don't listen, there is always the possibility that they themselves are to blame. It may simply be that too often they've said things not worth listening to. Yet, there are times when we all make it difficult for our bosses to listen to us. For example, we attempt to talk to them when they're on the run, in the middle of making a decision, or still mulling over in their minds the last conversation they had. How can we blame them for not listening when we hit them with new problems or ideas at such times?

Sometimes, too, we get so wrapped up with a subject we're discussing that we lose sight of the need to get a pertinent message across clearly and speedily. In an effort to build suspense or be climactic in letting the boss know how clever we were in handling a problem, we may put him or her to sleep. It's also very important to indicate to our listeners how our subject relates to them. If they get even the slightest feeling that what we are gabbing about is incidental, they are very likely to tune us out and begin thinking about something else.

Take a good look at how you have been communicating with Margaret. Are you guilty of one or more of the faults described above? A partial answer to why Margaret is a poor listener could very likely be here.

A good way to maintain communications with a boss who is not a good listener is to keep a file or diary of what was said, writing it immediately after each meeting. Date these notes to yourself and put them in a punch file so that you can later bring the subject up again or remind the boss of what was said or decided. Even bosses who are good listeners will appreciate this, especially those with lots of responsibilities. You may be commended for your concern and interest in the boss's welfare.

How a Supervisor Handled a Boss Who Was a Poor Listener

Richie A., supervisor in the marketing division of a business machines firm in New Jersey, learned that he could get his boss (Art R.) to listen to him only when the boss was in a receptive mood and Richie had his full attention. Consequently, he avoided bringing up an idea or a problem that he wanted to talk about until he had first warmed Art up by talking about another subject, one which he knew interested

Art—with Art, this subject was sports. Only when Richie saw that he had Art's full attention did he "get down to business." This casual prelude served another purpose. It clued Richie in to whether or not he had picked a good time for a particular conversation. If the boss seemed tense or distracted, he postponed his message or proposal to another time.

Perceiving when you have been heard is a valuable asset when you must communicate with a boss who is a poor listener. If you have doubts about getting through, bring the subject up again when you next meet.

The unreasonable boss who is always too busy to see you

The Problem

The keypunch operators you supervise in an insurance company's offices in Denver are working with the programmers in coding various accounts to a new-generation computer. Many problems have arisen with this project and you don't always have the solution. When you have tried to talk to your boss about them, he has put you off, saying, "See me later," or "You decide, I'm too busy." Such a brushoff wouldn't bother you if it happened only occasionally, but in the last few months it has occurred more and more frequently. The treatment has made you ill at ease because you've had to go to someone else for help, have held up a job, or have made a decision that the boss was responsible for. You hate to think that this practice will continue, but you can't foresee any change in the future. What should you do about the problem?

The Solution

Make an appointment to see the boss. He will probably not put you off when you come to his office and announce, "I'm here for our 9:00

meeting." Begin by saying that you realize he's been busy, but you feel that he should know that you are making some decisions that he might want to make. Be prepared to give at least one example. Then ask whether you're handling your job satisfactorily. This opening should prompt a discussion about why he has not given you help and guidance with your work. During the meeting, offer to help him with his duties, saying that it looks like he needs an assistant and that you would like to be it.

Bosses appreciate offers of help from their subordinates, particularly when they feel they are overworked. Specific suggestions of what you could do are especially good because they help the boss to determine which jobs to delegate. Bosses who are always too busy to see their people and work with them usually are guilty of not delegating as much as they should.

If you have not already done so, notice whether the boss treats other supervisors the same as he treats you. If you see that the boss is not too busy to see them, you can draw one of two conclusions: (1) he thinks very highly of you and feels you have the ability to do the job without his help or (2) he thinks you have been coming to him for help with decisions that *you* should make. Be honest with yourself in determining which is true. But also be aware that some bosses use the "too busy" ploy in order to push subordinates to be more aggressive and decisive.

One last point: unlikely as it may seem, you may have been a victim of circumstances several times when trying to see your boss. A too-busy boss should make it clear that timing is important.

How Another Supervisor Handled a Very Busy Boss

Katie B., supervisor of the buyers and expeditors of a department store chain, knew that she had to make the most of every opportunity she had to talk to her boss, Bernie F., because Bernie was always busy and gave her very little of his time. Accordingly, Katie was well prepared every time she stepped into the boss's office.

Katie always started by telling the boss what she was going to talk about—she gave him the punch line first. She then explained the subject clearly. Although she was tempted to give information in a nonstop fashion, she realized that such a procedure wouldn't let her know how much Bernie had heard, so from time to time she threw in a question such as, "Maybe another way would be better?" or "What do you think?" She also periodically compared several courses of action, pointing out which she thought best and asking for a reaction. Katie avoided asking questions that called for a simple yes or no answer. She tried to get Bernie to indicate how much of an impact Katie's comments had made. When the boss said something like, "I'll have to think about this," Katie replied, "Sure. But is there anything in particular that is causing you to hesitate about making the decision now?"

By preparing what she wanted to talk about, Katie saved the boss time. And by covering a lot of territory in an organized manner, she proved to the boss that she was an efficient supervisor.

11

The Untactful Boss

It's a human characteristic to want to be liked and respected. But when you work for a boss who lacks tact, you may have a tough time getting such attention. It's an unhappy fact that many supervisors work for bosses who are clumsy in expressing themselves, who don't follow the rules of etiquette, and who inflict scars of self-doubt on their people. What's worse, perhaps, is that such bosses often don't realize they are being indiscreet. Yet every supervisor should insist on his or her right to be treated reasonably and fairly, with respect and dignity.

In pursuit of such treatment, you must recognize that your boss may be under stress when he or she makes unkind remarks or handles a human relations problem poorly. You can help your own cause by steering the boss away from stressful situations and by preparing him or her for confrontations that may result in untactful behavior. Talking to the boss about the problem at an opportune time also helps.

The untactful boss who bypasses you

The Problem

The advertising agency you work for in New York is a leader in its industry, with a record number of accounts under contract. A fairly large staff is required to handle the accounts, and you and one other supervisor head up the two divisions in charge of the accounts. Both of you report to Henry M., a very aggressive, competitive individual who is continually on the go. He was responsible for the agency acquiring several new accounts last month, two of which were assigned to your division.

Last week, Henry bypassed you and went directly to the people you had assigned to the new accounts. In one case, he asked that a market research study be made immediately. A few days later he told one of your account executives to prepare some sketches for approval. You learned of the first incident when your subordinate came to you for help, and you ran across the other accidentally when passing by the account executive's desk.

Should you overlook Henry's giving assignments directly to your people because of his original involvement with those accounts? If he continues to bypass you and you decide to talk to him about it, what should you say?

The Solution

Go to Henry and tell him what you discovered. Acknowledge that you know he is deeply interested in those accounts. Say that you are aware he means well, but that when he bypasses you, he undermines your authority as well as confuses your people. Explain that this makes it difficult for you to give them assignments because they feel strongly obligated to put his requests ahead of everything else. Conclude by saying that you would appreciate it if he talked to only you when he wanted a job done.

An alternative way of handling Henry and getting your message across is to tell him that you just found out that one of your people is working on a job that he gave him. Ask Henry if he would like to have you drop the job you gave the man or if his job can wait until your job is finished.

Some bosses will bypass their subordinates and then tell them about it afterward. Reporting after the fact apparently relieves their conscience. There really isn't a good way to combat the practice, except perhaps by frowning while thanking the boss for telling you.

In small companies or in closely knit organizations, bosses are prone to do a lot of bypassing and not much is thought of it. Managerial people may be scarce and supervisors may wear several hats. Responsibilities may overlap considerably and people may take orders from more than one boss. This can lead to trouble when there are differences of opinion or when bosses at different levels are inconsiderate toward one another.

Most bosses in large organizations, however, agree that requests to get work done or jobs handled should follow the chain of command. The bosses that violate the unwritten rule are usually the overzealous, eager, and impatient ones who see an opportunity to save time or who fear that something will be lost in the communication step.

How Another Supervisor Handled the Bypassing Problem

Brian J., supervisor of the computer programmers in a food processing company in Los Angeles, recognized soon after being promoted to the position that his boss, Andrew Z., was the type of manager who could be expected to bypass supervisors. Andrew had a strong interest in computers and information retrieval. Brian knew from what he'd heard about his boss that it would be difficult if not impossible to change the man. Accordingly, in a staff meeting with his department, Brian brought up the subject of Andrew's tendency to bypass supervisors. Brian asked his subordinates to give the boss's requests the highest priority, but to *immediately* tell Brian what Andrew had requested. By handling the problem in this manner, Brian was able to guide his people on those assignments, make adjustments to his own work schedule, and know which direction his boss felt the department should be going in.

You can save yourself a confrontation with your boss if you're willing to overlook his or her tactlessness. Unfortunately, you may lose status in the eyes of some of your people. But those of your people who understand—the ones that really matter—will think nothing of it.

The untactful boss who treats you disrespectfully

The Problem

You are the supervisor for a cross-country trucking company whose largest terminal is located on the south side of Chicago. Your people are members of a union whose local branch is very strong, particularly in the influence it has on the operations at your terminal. You and your boss meet frequently with the union representatives to discuss working conditions and complaints of the employees.

Your boss, W. Brown, doesn't enjoy these meetings and tries to make them as short as possible. He frequently is able to do this by agreeing that the employees are justified in complaining and by promising to take action to correct inequities or improve conditions. Although he does not always keep his promises, this doesn't bother you. What does irk you is that he blames the problems and the poor conditions on you. Remarks such as, "If I had a good supervisor, you fellows would not have to put up with that," and, "Frank, why haven't you handled this?" make you look bad. In many cases, what he blames you for is not your responsibility.

What should you do about this situation and the way the boss treats you?

The Solution

The next time Brown disparages you publicly, ask if you can talk with him privately for a few minutes. Ask him if he meant to treat you disrespectfully by what he said. Depending on how he replies, tell him that if he has no respect for you, you'd like to know why, so you can earn it. If he claims that he does respect you, ask why you get the feeling that he doesn't.

If he again makes disparaging remarks about you in a union meeting, talk to him afterward. Say something along these lines: "I need your support in dealing with some of my people and the union. If you don't show me any respect, they won't either, and my job will be that much more difficult."

A boss who treats workers disrespectfully doesn't understand the importance of good human relations. You can sometimes help such a boss by talking with him or her about people problems; describe what you've learned from your experiences and explain how you try to handle specific situations. If you can get the boss to listen and think about such incidents before he makes a comment or acts, he or she may learn to be more tactful. You might adopt such a procedure for your meetings with the union representatives. Since you both know in general what is going to be discussed, sit down before the meeting and work out your strategy. The boss can have his answers to complaints in mind and not have to resort to unkind remarks on the spur of the moment.

If Brown shows disrespect for you privately, you should immediately ask, "Are you annoyed with me for some reason?" If he says that he isn't and wants to know why you've asked, say, "Well, you talk to me differently when you're pleased with my work, so I wondered what was wrong."

How Another Supervisor Handled a Similar Problem

Dennis R., supervisor of the planners and expediters at a materials supply house in Dallas, Texas, was at first shocked and then dismayed when his boss showed no respect for him in a meeting with management. Dennis was not at the meeting—he learned about his boss's remarks from a close friend who was there. Dennis' boss, Jason, stated that Dennis was not aggressive enough in dealing with contractors and suppliers, that he too often took the side of the outsiders in disputes, and that he was too willing to compromise when the company was clearly in the right. Rather than betray his friend by confronting Jason about his remarks, Dennis began a self-improvement program. He began going to bat for his people and helping them with their problems. He stopped being a "yes man" in his dealings with contractors and suppliers, and adopted a "yes-but" technique with his boss. Although it took time, he eventually was looked upon more favorably by his boss.

The untactful boss who doesn't give you credit

The Problem

You are a supervisor in a large brokerage firm in New York City. Your responsibilities include seeing that the brokers are daily provided with data and information on securities and that they follow company policy in dealing with customers. You are also their source of information on transactions that are out of the ordinary or require special handling. Consolidation of the firm's activities for reporting to government agencies is another of your many responsibilities.

At the present time, you feel insecure on the job because your boss, C. White, seldom, if ever, gives you credit for your accomplishments. White is a reticent person who rarely ventures out of his office. In his communications with you he is usually short and to the point. You don't recall ever getting a compliment from him, even when you brought the firm additional business through a unique arrangement you worked out with one of the firm's large accounts. In addition, you have not had a raise in pay for a long time.

What should you do about receiving credit for what you do? How do you go about getting a raise from White?

The Solution

Be assured that you are not alone in feeling that you deserve credit for what you do on the job. Unfortunately, too many bosses fail to see the need to tell their subordinates that what they do is recognized and appreciated.

The best way to get recognition is to publicize your efforts and accomplishments. Talk to White about your work. Suggest that you submit a weekly report that includes a summary of the problems your department has encountered and a brief description of the way you and your people resolved those problems. Expand this report to include your analysis of specific situations and a survey of current trends. Sell your suggestion by showing how such a report could provide valuable information to him as well as keep him up to date on the activities of the brokers. Mention that the report would also be of value as a historical document in the firm's files.

Set a good example. Tell the boss when one of your people has a significant accomplishment. Let the boss know that you complimented the fellow and that you noticed that the compliment was appreciated.

As for getting a raise, you might try pleading your cause by using someone else as a point of reference. For example, you may direct your boss's attention to one of your worthy brokers who deserves a raise, stating merits that closely parallel those you feel you have yourself. This maneuver is a sort of transfer of communication in that you attribute your own situation to another. Astute bosses pick this up and make an adjustment, if in retrospect they see you deserve it.

How Another Supervisor Earned Recognition

Walter S., supervisor of a bridge repair crew in Michigan, worked hard and took pride in his accomplishments. He was ambitious and hoped to have his own business some day. His immediate goal, however, was to get a better job with the contractor he worked for and to receive more pay. The problem was that he wasn't sure his boss recognized his capabilities and his contribution to the company. Walter came up with a plan to remedy that situation.

After completing each repair, no matter how large or small, he made a point of touching base with his boss to discuss the job. In those meetings he asked the boss questions relative to the job such as, "We finished that job quite a few days ahead of schedule, didn't we?" or, "How did you like the way we got around the bad weather?" or, "I guess the county was pleased with our work, weren't they?"

Walter's boss soon recognized the need to give him credit for what he and his crew had accomplished and to increase his pay. With that, Walter had made one of the steps to his future success.

The untactful boss who frequently embarrasses you

The Problem

You are the supervisor in a heavy machinery manufacturing plant in New Haven, Connecticut. It is an old firm, and many of the mechanics and machinists who work for you have many years of experience. Even with your mechanical engineering degree, it's difficult for you to keep up with them. Your boss, Carl R., also is a mechanical engineer and at one time held your job. Carl likes to get out in the plant and in the maintenance shop to relive the days when he was supervisor. Unfortunately, he often embarrasses you in front of your department. He may criticize the work procedure you have specified or question your use of particular materials. He has also called you down for taking too long to get a machine repaired and back in service. Such criticism bothers you, especially when your workers hear it. What should you do about this lack of tact in your boss?

The Solution

Ask Carlson if he is aware that he has criticized and embarrassed you in front of your subordinates. Ask him if he knows how this affects you and if he's aware of how it looks to the people who work for you. Then say that you wish he would try not to do it. If you talk in a calm manner and show that you are truly concerned, the boss may apologize.

If you are loyal to your boss and do a good job, you have a right to expect that he or she will not embarrass you. Unfortunately, bosses with tough skins are inclined to dismiss the matter when you call it to their attention, mainly because they are not easily embarrassed themselves. But suppose your boss continues to embarrass you after you have talked about it. There is one more step you can take: the next time the boss asks you to accompany him or her to a meeting at which he or she might embarrass you, gracefully decline saying, "Thank you, but I'd rather not. I'm afraid you'll embarrass me with these people." That remark should sink deep.

The fact that a supervisor may be embarrassed by a boss does not lower the supervisor's status in the eyes of subordinates or hinder his or her ability to handle subordinates. Quite the contrary, it usually raises the supervisor's rating because the embarrassment signifies that he or she has high standards and morals. There would be no embarrassment if it were not so. Remember too that good supervisors never let their standards slip in an attempt to avoid embarrassment.

How Another Supervisor Handled Embarrassment

Harry K., supervisor of the order clerks at a publishing company in West Nyack, New York, was very conscientious about his work and always tried to do his best. He couldn't understand why his boss frequently spoke to him sarcastically and rudely in front of other people. Although he realized that his boss was discourteous only when he was under pressure, Harry resented such treatment. He decided he had to let the boss know how he felt, but he wanted to be subtle about it.

The next time the boss rudely gave him an order in front of a clerk, Harry let him finish what he had to say and then left, telling the boss he wanted to think about it back at his desk. Then, unless the order was very important, he didn't do what the boss asked for. When the boss later asked him why he didn't handle the matter, Harry told him that he hadn't been able to decide what to do because he didn't fully understand what the boss wanted. He explained that the boss must have been under strain because he didn't give his order calmly and privately, and this confused Harry. Thereafter, the boss gave his orders politely to Harry when he was not with other employees.

12

When Your Ideas Are Not Accepted

Every supervisor sometimes suffers the frustration of not having an idea accepted. Whether your people, the boss, a troublemaker in the department, or a loyal employee reject you or your idea, damage is done to your ego. In addition to being disappointed, you may lose confidence in yourself and your abilities. You may also question the logic and judgment of the person who doesn't agree with you, but that, of course, doesn't solve your problem.

As soon as you learn that your idea is not accepted, find out why. Many reasons are possible, depending on who is not accepting you and why that person does not agree with you. Some people, such as your boss, will tell you, but most of the others will not. They will simply ignore you, continue their usual practice, and let you learn for yourself. You can't ignore nonacceptance of your ideas if you expect to be a success and move up in your company.

When your ideas are not accepted by subordinates

The Problem

You supervise the erection crew in a food processing plant in Michigan. Since the business is seasonal, many of the employees are new and inexperienced when the plant begins to operate in June of each year. Consequently, you are very busy instructing and training crew members on overhauling old equipment as well as installing new. You are continually making arrangements for tools and materials. Frequent product changes during the season lead to much confusion.

Your biggest concern, however, is that many workers have their own ideas about how permanent the installations should be, since they know that a product change will require them to relocate or modify the equipment. Veteran employees remember how the job was done last year; new employees think they know a better way. Downtime must always be kept to a minimum and job priorities must be established. Your workers are not always willing to work overtime on short notice. What should you do to have more order and less indecision in the work area? How can you display the attributes of a leader and have your ideas accepted without question?

The Solution

You have a tough supervisory job. The only way to successfully handle it is to be well organized and to plan your work in advance as much as possible. The best way to give instructions and to demonstrate how you want a job done is to instruct crew members at the job site—and then stay there until everyone agrees how the job is to be done.

Get to know the capabilities of your people. You have to know what each worker can do before assigning him or her a task. You also have to know enough about a job to assign it to a particular person. Crew members soon lose confidence in the supervisor who assigns a pipefitter, a mechanic, and a laborer to a job that requires only the mechanic. Before matching craftspeople to specific jobs, compare their abilities to the tasks. Then expand the list of skills available as the crew gains experience working on different equipment. Overhauls and major jobs require careful thought and planning. You have to consider the needs of the production department. Plan on completing a major job by a certain date and with the shortest possible downtime.

To have people available when you need them, make arrangements in advance and follow the plant's priority system. The production department should set priorities. Expect that you may have to coordinate tools, material, and rigging each day.

There is an advantage to not telling your people exactly how a job should be done. They will have more interest in their work and take more pride in it if some of the decisions are theirs. But you should do this only with experienced people. Pair a new craftsperson with an experienced one on two-person jobs. After you demonstrate to people that you know their capabilities, you understand the jobs, and you've planned the work, you will find that you are truly in charge and your ideas will be accepted.

How Another Supervisor Handled Nonacceptance of Ideas

Keith R., supervisor of the rate adjusters in an insurance office, thought he was moving up to an easy job when he was promoted to that position. But after a few weeks on the job, he realized that he was wrong. The rate adjusters seemed to ignore him much of the time, seldom came to him with their problems, and in general seemed unwilling to cooperate. When one of the men went to Keith's superior to confirm an instruction, Keith realized that he had to do something about improving his communications skills.

He began by talking with the adjusters the first thing in the morning before they became involved in their jobs. When policy changes were pending, he tried to focus on what the change meant to the adjusters and to policy holders. Keith presented not only the company's side of a controversial issue, but other viewpoints as well, generally letting the rate adjusters see all the factors involved. He never harped on a subject—he tried to close the discussion before interest waned. And he didn't try to do the whole job of keeping his people informed himself; he often arranged for group meetings with *his* boss. It wasn't long before he was better accepted and found it easier to get a message across.

When your ideas are not accepted by your boss

The Problem

Hal T., supervisor in the training division of an automotive company in Detroit, had been an instructor in the division for five years. When the division recently expanded and began training more employees, Hal was a logical choice to be named supervisor because of his capability, experience, and enthusiasm. Determined to be a success in his new job, Hal felt that he could contribute most by revising some of the courses and injecting new ideas into others. Accordingly, he worked up a proposal of his ideas for management's approval, selecting an area that he felt most needed improvement.

But Hal was disappointed when his boss turned down the proposal, saying that it was too theoretical. Hal went to work on a second proposal, determined to give the boss what he wanted and making sure it was practical. He presented a problem that the company had encountered some time ago and showed what decisions would have been made using the analytic methods he proposed. Then he compared his proposed results with the actual course of action taken. With this approach, he was able to clearly show the advantages of using his proposal.

Again Hal's idea was not accepted. This time his boss explained that hindsight is good when it's applied strictly to events in the past, but there's no guarantee that a procedure that might have worked well some time ago will work well today. What should Hal do so that more of his ideas will be accepted by his boss?

The Solution

Hal should realize that his boss is uncomfortable with theoretical discussions—apparently he is distrustful of a concept he hasn't seen applied. Hal's boss is unimpressed by specific solutions to past problems, unless there is evidence that the same solution would work for a current problem. The answer is to prepare a proposal that would be a blend of the general and the specific, that would be supported by evidence not only from the past but also from the present. At each step Hal should bring his point home with an illustration or example. To conclude, he should compare results under the old and new methods, thus fortifying his case.

Hal should also try to give his boss a vested interest in a new idea. This is accomplished by including his suggestions and recognizing his contributions. When bosses feel that you are expressing their ideas as part or in support of yours, they are more likely to accept the whole package. Hal should recognize too, that there is power in numbers. If others in the department agree with an idea, Hal should let the boss know. Astute supervisors get help from others when they have a tough problem to solve or an important idea to sell.

When presenting ideas, making a speech, or submitting a written report, you must always keep in mind the personality of your boss and the way he or she thinks. Your material should be slanted accordingly. And when you present concepts and generalizations, always support them with specific examples.

How Another Supervisor Fostered Acceptance of Her Ideas

Betty K., supervisor of the designers and set-up people with a major public relations firm in New York, had carefully worked out a new PR plan. She perfected every detail and anticipated every objection, and then couldn't sell her plan to her boss. This had happened to her several times and Betty began to wonder what was wrong. Were her ideas too far out? Did she do a poor job of explaining them? Did she catch the boss at bad times?

Looking back, Betty suddenly realized that the rejections came when she asked for approval of an idea immediately after she had presented it. By pressing for an immediate answer, she had not permitted her boss time to think about, investigate, and consider her proposal. Thereafter, whenever Betty had an idea or suggestion to offer her boss, she would say, "Why don't you think about this for a while? I don't want your answer today." She found that by handling her ideas this way, more of them were accepted.

To work more effectively with your boss and get your ideas accepted, you should allow him or her to review and consider them for a while. This may take a few hours, a day, or even a week, depending on how busy your boss is and the priority given to your proposal. After all, you shouldn't expect someone to reason out in a brief period what may have taken you weeks or a month to think through.

When your ideas are not accepted by a troublemaker

The Problem

"Dusty" Rhodes is a truck driver for a freight line operating in the Midwest. In the eyes of management, he is a belligerent fellow who is out for all he can get and who always has a complaint of one type or another. He feels that truck drivers are taken advantage of by freight line companies and has several times encouraged his fellow drivers to complain about working conditions and to refuse to accept the schedules. Last week Rhodes didn't like your suggestion that he inspect his rig and check off the operation of the controls before leaving the truck terminal on a trip. He stated that this job should be handled by the terminal's maintenance people, and that drivers should be given rigs in top-notch condition. As Rhodes' supervisor, what should you do about him? Should you threaten to suspend him if he doesn't accept your ideas or orders? He will certainly try to persuade the other drivers to take his side if you press the issue.

The Solution

Sympathizing with complainers sometimes helps to mollify them. However, Rhodes has apparently progressed beyond the complaining stage—he may begin to cause serious trouble. Troublemakers expect the reaction they normally get. By threatening to suspend Rhodes, you may be giving him just what he wants. Hostile, aggressive people are often experts at making a trivial matter a major one. The best way to handle such people is to let them complain and blow off steam, but don't give them a reason to explode. Unless your management says that drivers *must* inspect their rigs, you would be wise to back off on this suggestion.

Of course, that doesn't apply when you give Rhodes an order that is covered by company policy or rules of behavior. Here you must insist that he carry out your order or suffer the consequences of discipline. In unionized companies, an employee can turn in a complaint or grievance if he or she feels an order is unfair, is unjust, or violates the union–management agreement. But, even in such cases, the employee is expected to do what his or her supervisor requests at the moment.

Fear is not high on the list of motivators in today's labor climate. But if all of your attempts to get Rhodes to be more cooperative fail, it may be your only alternative. Unfortunately, with some troublemakers, confronting them with the ultimate consequences is the only language they seem to understand. Fear may be worth a try with Rhodes. You could tell him to either shape up or get out. If concern about losing his job fails to change him, you may have no option left but to recommend that he be fired.

If you take the time to analyze troublemakers, you will discover that they are simply resisting conformity. Every troublemaker is negative in some respect. They exhibit that negativism whenever a plan or idea is presented to them. Unless that plan is exactly what they wanted or hoped for, they will look for reasons to oppose or reject it. You've got to show them how they can benefit from a new idea.

How Another Supervisor Handled an Uncooperative Employee

Albert B., supervisor of a group of draftsmen in an engineering consulting firm in New Jersey, got along well with his workers, with one exception. "Whitey" W., an older fellow, seemed to resent Albert as his supervisor. Albert took this rejection personally until he noticed that Whitey cooperated with only one co-worker, a draftsman. When searching for why these two fellows got along well, he learned that they shared a common hobby: collecting coins. Albert began to read up on the subject and then casually discussed it one day with Whitey's friend. The next thing he knew, Whitey shared with him his luck at finding a rather rare coin. From that time on, Albert and he occasionally talked about coins; Whitey was much more cooperative and no longer made critical remarks about the work or his assignments.

Supervisors cannot afford to let an individual's rejection or criticism worry them. However, when many people are criticizing, it could mean that something is wrong. Then they should look into the problem and take corrective action.

When your ideas are not accepted by a conscientious employee

The Problem

Alma R. is an environmental officer in a government agency in Washington, D.C. She has been with the agency for five years and has always been a loyal employee—she makes a sincere effort to perform well. To do this consistently requires that she keep up to date on regulations and follow up on inspections and communications. This is not easy for Alma because many of the regulations are complex and detailed. It is difficult to always interpret them as the legislators intended and Alma needs help in doing this. You realize that Alma respects you as her supervisor because she comes to you for help when she has an unusual problem. But in the last few months there have been several occasions when Alma didn't follow your orders and instructions, with the result that problems were not completely solved or individuals and companies were unhappy with the agency's ruling. What should you do about Alma's failure to accept and carry out your orders?

The Solution

Almost every supervisor at one time or another has been victimized by improper implementation of his or her instructions. While the supervisor may be inclined to find fault with a subordinate when problems occur as a result, most often it is the supervisor's own fault.

If you spell out the details of assignments with Alma, you must include everything. Any omission can result in a delay or a bad decision. You are responsible for anticipating every contingency. Step-by-step instructions are easier to follow, and there will be fewer unexpected problems if you give assignments that specify the results desired. But you must be certain that Alma really understands what you want. Have her tell you—in her own words—what you have asked her to do. This will give you a chance to prevent a misunderstanding and to be sure that you've not forgotten something.

Look for other reasons why Alma hasn't carried out your orders. Have you been tense or under stress? If you were cold or gruff when giving her assignments she may not have heard you properly. What about Alma's mental and physical condition? Was she upset or ill during the time your problems developed? Check out these possibilities.

How a Supervisor Solved the Problem
of Ignored Instructions

Gloria F., supervisor of the machine operators in a bank in downtown Chicago, was dedicated and determined to improve the productivity of people in her department. After a period of time however, she felt that she was pushing too much. Her subordinates were beginning to resent her close, constant supervision. When one of the younger employees responded with a sharp remark one day, Gloria realized that she herself might be the problem, especially when her orders and instructions were not followed.

After analyzing her approach on the job, Gloria saw that she often interrupted people under the guise of following up. The interruption invariably interfered with the person's concentration on a task. Since it took the person more than a few minutes to get back into the job, the total output of that person was less. Gloria also realized that she occasionally kept people waiting when she neglected to make sure that machines were available for use before she assigned people to operate them. When several of her people had to stop working and locate her to ask for clarification of instructions, Gloria realized that some of her orders were poorly worded, subject to misunderstanding, or given in haste, a poor way to communicate. Fortunately, Gloria recognized her failings and decided to do something about them. A few months later her habits had changed and she was better accepted by her people.

Whenever you find that your ideas are not accepted, it is time to rate yourself—remember, your supervisory performance is not rated only by your boss. Don't overlook the fact that supervisors are discussed, rated, and compared by their subordinates. Such reviews and rankings won't appear in your personnel file, but they'll show up during work breaks, at lunch, and whenever you mismanage a work assignment.

13

Being Fair

Supervising involves working with people, instructing them, and giving them orders. Through these functions, you manage and get work done by other people. How successful you are in carrying out these and other supervisory responsibilities depends partly on how fair you are and partly on how fair people *think* you are.

Convincing people that you are fair is important because unhappy, disappointed, angry, or disgruntled people do not perform at their best and are less willing to cooperate. People will more readily accept your decisions if you are honest with them and if you explain your words and actions and are not biased or prejudiced. To do this, you must constantly put yourself in the other person's shoes when you instruct or give an order. With experience, you will learn that when you treat people fairly you will be treated fairly in return.

Being fair when you make assignments

The Problem

You are a supervisor for a contractor specializing in equipment installations in the Houston, Texas, area. The company supplies labor mainly to the chemicals industry. You handle one of several crews that do preparatory work, install piping and equipment, and test the system before turning it over to the customer.

In recent months, business has been very competitive because chemicals companies have made fewer capital investments. With a scarcity of work for craftsmen, your company has had to cut costs in order to get contracts. Crews have been reduced in number and in size. Your boss has told you to keep your people busy. This afternoon, "Hank" Hankins, a mechanic, finished installing a pump early in the afternoon and you had no other mechanical work to assign him. Since the forms around the pump foundation had not been removed nor had scrap material been taken from the area, you asked Hankins to do this work. He protested, saying that he was a mechanic and his job description didn't cover removing forms or cleaning up. What should you do under the circumstances? What should you say to Hankins?

The Solution

Tell Hankins that he is being paid for a full day's work and that's what he should give the company. Point out that unless all employees help to hold costs down, the company will not get jobs in the area. And when there is no work, the company will be forced to lay off people.

If you read Hankins' job description carefully, you will probably find that the work you asked him to do falls under the category of "work incidental to carrying out the main responsibility," or some similar category. Inform him of this and explain that management is entitled to use idle craftsmen as constructively and productively as possible. Show him that by doing the work he will not deprive any other employee of a job.

Although some workers may think that you are not being fair when you assign them work that they usually don't do, loyal as well as honest employees will agree that this is your responsibility when an employee is idle. The problem of idle people is a difficult one for many supervisors in that they must avoid showing favoritism in assigning other work. Be sure you don't give easy jobs to people whom you think will protest tough ones. Also, distribute the distasteful work among all your people.

Studies by psychologists have shown that people on the job try to meet the expectations of supervisors whom they know to have high ethical standards. When working for an honest person, it is difficult to be dishonest. If a person is fair to you, you tend to be fair to him.

How Another Supervisor Was Fair in Making Assignments

Harry S., supervisor of the pipefitters in a refinery in Beaumont, Texas, assigned his people jobs in pairs, as was the custom in the industry. Most of the work was heavy and much of it involved handling large pipe. He was surprised, therefore, when Pete F., a quiet but excellent worker, asked for jobs that he could work at alone. Knowing that Pete was honest and sincere, Harry agreed, even though it was against normal procedures in the plant. Some of the other pipefitters accused Harry of being a slave driver until he explained and Pete confirmed the agreement. The change proved to benefit everyone because Pete quickly demonstrated that he could handle many jobs just as efficiently as two pipefitters usually did and he preferred to work by himself.

You may mistakenly think of lone workers as being people who prefer to be physically separated from other people on the job. Although some people are of this nature, most "loners" simply prefer not to interact with others or be team members. They want to work *in* groups rather than *with* groups. They prefer to be inconspicuous. Supervisors should accede to such people's desires as much as company rules and regulations will allow in order to be fair to them.

Being fair when you criticize someone

The Problem

Dorothy C., order clerk in a trucking firm office in Toledo, Ohio, made two serious errors last week. As a result, one shipment was sent to the wrong address and another was shipped two days late. Both errors came to your boss's attention when customers complained. The boss has asked you, Dorothy's supervisor, to talk to her about the errors and do whatever is necessary to prevent their recurrence. You don't remember the last time that Dorothy made an error, and naturally, you hope that she will not continue to make them. What's the best way of going about this? How should you talk to her? You want to be fair but you must also let Dorothy know that such errors are serious.

The Solution

When you approach Dorothy to discuss the problem, remember that the purpose of criticism should be three-fold: (1) to prevent a recurrence of some pattern of behavior, (2) to teach better ways, and (3) to increase efficiency. To be most effective, commend first, criticize in private, remain calm, get all the facts, and be constructive. If you faithfully follow these rules, you will be as fair as you can be under the circumstances.

Nobody enjoys being criticized. It wounds our pride, undermines our sense of importance, and sometimes arouses our resentment. By praising first, you take the sting out of what is to follow. Assure Dorothy that you still have great regard for her and imply that you recognize her errors as a departure from her usual good performance.

Talk to Dorothy in private. Private criticism always gets better results than public criticism, and your listener will appreciate your effort to not embarrass him or her. Also, stay calm. While blowing your top about Dorothy's errors may make you feel better, it will not prevent a recurrence nor will it teach her a better way. Most of the facts you seek must come from Dorothy, and the best way to encourage her to tell you about the problem is to ask the simple question, "What happened?" It boils the whole issue down to *what* went wrong rather than *who* is to blame or *why* she did it. With personalities eliminated, you should get straight answers. The facts will tell you what the real problem is.

Keep your criticism constructive. Most people want to feel important, and everybody has pride. There is no good purpose served by tearing Dorothy down. Telling someone that he or she is stupid isn't criticism at all. Working with a person to learn from a mistake or error and to prevent it from happening again is positive, purposeful criticism. It's also the only kind that works.

How One Supervisor Put Fairness Ahead of Criticism

Henry R., supervisor for a tobacco company in Kentucky, was a firm believer in letting his people know how they stood with him. He kept in close contact with them, frequently reviewed their progress, and kept them informed about the status of problem situations. One of his most irksome concerns was the performance of a packaging machine operator, Joe T. Joe had been passed over for merit increases in pay several times over the past few years while younger and less experienced operators had received increases as well as promotions. He had been a marginal employee from the start, and his productivity had declined over the years to the point where his work was no longer satisfactory. Henry had occasionally given Joe minimal wage increases, no more than cost-of-living raises. But each time, Henry had had to decide whether to give Joe the increase or take steps to have him transferred or discharged.

When performance evaluation time came around this year, Henry was faced once again with the same decision.

After giving the matter a lot of thought, he decided that evaluating Joe's performance wasn't likely to have any constructive effect, and that there was no point in wasting his time or Joe's on criticism. The biggest favor that Henry could do for the company, and quite possibly for Joe as well, was to recommend to his superior that Joe be discharged. That was his decision, and Henry's superior agreed that it was a good one.

The only time that criticism is useful is when it provides an opportunity for growth. If you see that criticizing one of your people will be to no avail, hold up on it. You will be fairer to both the person and the company if you choose another course of action.

Being fair when you must discipline an employee

The Problem

Your company is one of the largest in the life insurance field and most of its records and operations are computerized. Because information must enter the data base promptly and correctly, the position of key-punch operator is an important one in the company. One of your key-punch operators, Cheryl S., has been with the department for over a year and has done a good job in that time. But she has an attendance problem. She was absent several days last month and on three separate days this month, handicapping your department. When you discussed her absences with her, she offered a different reason each time, none of which included illness. You feel that you must break this pattern, disciplining her if necessary, but you want to be fair and just about it. What should you do? How do you impose discipline for poor attendance?

The Solution

Since you have already orally discussed Cheryl's absences with her to apparently no avail, your next step is to give her a written warning.

The letter should state that failure to improve her attendance would subject her to disciplinary action. Make sure a copy of the letter goes in her file in the personnel department.

Consult with your boss on company policy for handling absenteeism. The company should have a disciplinary procedure that every supervisor follows. If your company doesn't have such a policy, ask your boss to establish one for your department and have it posted.

To be effective, discipline must be (1) uniform, (2) corrective, and (3) progressive. Discipline must be uniform: The same offense should not elicit a written warning from one supervisor and a suspension from another. A written policy prevents such inequities.

Be sure your discipline is corrective, not punitive. Absenteeism is a correctable offense and ample opportunity for correction is usually granted. In corrective discipline, proper conduct is described and an offender is given the opportunity to correct his or her improper conduct the next time the same or a similar situation arises. Such discipline warns other employees that misconduct or rule-breaking will subject them to disciplinary action.

Discipline is progressive when penalties for repeated offenses are made more severe step by step. Typically, an oral warning is followed by a written warning, a one-day suspension without pay, a five-day suspension without pay, and a discharge. Similar offenses of the same severity should have the same number of steps, the number varying with the severity of the action. While fighting, for example, usually results in a two- or three-step discharge, absenteeism requires more steps.

You should not be thinking about firing Cheryl. Turnover costs money in hiring, training, and loss of output. If Cheryl can correct her conduct after minor discipline, you save the company turnover costs. Besides, you know the qualities and abilities of Cheryl; you cannot be sure of the qualities and abilities of her replacement.

How Another Supervisor Handled Absenteeism

Robert A., supervisor in a furniture factory in Alabama where absenteeism was becoming an increasing problem, participated when his company set a policy for handling it. He became involved when one of the people in his department, Roger K., was discharged after repeated requests to improve unsatisfactory attendance. However, the union took the matter to arbitration and Roger was reinstated after the arbitrator ruled the penalty too severe. The arbitrator reasoned that although the employee had received written warnings about absenteeism, none had been issued during the four months prior to his discharge. In reality, the company lost because discipline was not progressive. Had progressive procedures been followed, the penalty should have been suspension, not discharge, the arbitrator said.

After this incident, Robert and the personnel manager of the company set up a point system under which a worker was charged one point for each absence. After receiving a certain number of points, the final penalty was discharge. The absentee rate in the factory quickly dropped. The point system was effective because it was fair, reasonable, and progressive.

Being fair when judging the work of employees

The Problem

You are supervisor of the methods department of a paint and coating company in Cleveland, Ohio. Your company recently required that all managers conduct performance appraisals with their subordinates. The company hopes that the practice will cause employees to improve their skills and become more productive on the job.

Last week your boss talked with you about your performance. Afterward, he reminded you to schedule conferences with each of the people in your department. You are not looking forward to this job, for several reasons. You question your ability to properly judge other people's work. You are worried that people will think you are not fair. You realize that you are going to have to tell a technician, Stacey R., that much of his work is below standard and unacceptable.

How do you go about convincing people that you are fair when conducting a performance appraisal? What, specifically, should you say to Stacey?

The Solution

First, be assured that no one in your company is better suited to judge your people's work than yourself. If Stacey has been working for you for very long, you should be aware of capabilities and his weaknesses and you should know whether he is a responsible individual. You already have judged him to some extent: You believe that much of his work is below standard for the position.

Convincing people you are fair is important when you are conducting a performance appraisal, but it is even more important in your daily interactions with them. If you praise one person more than another when they have both completed a job satisfactorily, you're guilty of favoritism. It's only natural to like some people more than others, but you should try not to show your feelings by giving special treatment to certain people. If you assign someone a job that is beyond that person's capabilities, it isn't fair to expect a perfect job. Keep that in mind when you hand out work and when you judge performance.

Your employees expect to be given credit for good work. You should recommend merit raises for outstanding performance and compliment your people as well. If productive employees discover that others less industrious or less qualified have received those special benefits, your fairness is sure to be questioned. At times, you and someone you supervise may have different opinions on a subject. If you're unsympathetic to opinions that differ from your own, you're apt to be seen as unfair. Try to be open-minded and deal with people on the basis of what they've done, not what they profess or how they feel.

When talking to Stacey, be frank and honest. Tell him that his work is unsatisfactory without qualifications. While you might say that "it is satisfactory but needs some changes," it is better that you be entirely honest in order that you not hold back his development and advancement. Stacey will be better able to know what is expected of him if he gets the truth.

Supervisors are being fair when they make decisions on the basis of facts and conditions rather than on emotions. To be fair, they must avoid being swayed by personalities and actions of individuals; they must think and act objectively.

How a Supervisor Judged a Person's Work Unfairly

Supervisor Pat N. had a reputation for being a tough but technically competent boss of the technicians at a research center in Columbus, Ohio. He frequently stated that supervision wasn't a popularity contest and that he was going to run a well-controlled operation. But he had been on the job for only six months when he ran into trouble. Turnover in the department had increased since he had taken over and two of the department's best technicians had resigned to accept jobs with competitive organizations. Pat's boss, Ralph J., disturbed by the high turnover, began to investigate the situation.

Ralph agreed that running a tight, no-nonsense operation was not the best way to become popular. In his experience, however, a competent and fair-minded supervisor who insisted on high standards of performance was generally liked by his better-performing people. After asking Pat's permission, Ralph talked to the people in Pat's department and studied the problem. He learned that one of the technicians had resigned because Pat had criticized him too harshly.

Ralph told Pat that it's a common pitfall for inexperienced supervisors to be too severe in their judgments and to judge the person rather than his or her specific behavior. Criticism is beneficial only when it is given objectively and impersonally.

Being fair when you must say no

The Problem

Roberta S. is the word processing specialist in the office services department that you supervise. The workload in the department fluctuates with the number of clients your public relations firm has to serve, and this varies from day to day and week to week. On some days Roberta has very little work to do, while on others you've had to ask her to work overtime to get out a rush job. She has always been cooperative and understanding, and has never refused to do what you've asked of her.

Earlier this week Roberta asked you for a day's vacation on Friday. She explained that her parents would be in town and that she was planning a full day of activities with them. Since the office workload was light, you granted her request. But this morning, Thursday, an important client asked for some releases that require Roberta's skill. There is more than a day's work involved and the releases are needed immediately. How do you break the bad news to Roberta?

The Solution

Much as you may dislike doing it, you must immediately tell Roberta that she will have to work tomorrow. Naturally, she is going to be very unhappy. Try to soften the blow and to help by looking for a way that something might be salvaged from the situation. Perhaps some of the work can be done Thursday afternoon or evening. See if she could be spared on Friday afternoon by having the client wait until Monday for some of the releases.

Of course, you must fully explain what happened and why you must reverse yourself on letting her have the day off. Use the kindest words you know and show that you understand her feelings on the matter. People do not like to be turned down. They hope and usually expect to get what they ask for, and some people may be argumentative when you say *no*. But when a refusal is the proper and only answer you can give, be sure you explain why.

Saying *no* is usually difficult. It runs counter to positive thinking, enthusiasm, and cooperation—all the means of getting along with people and getting a job done. Put on a smile when you must say *no*. Doing that makes it easier on everybody.

How Another Supervisor Said No

Hal R., supervisor of the Parks and Recreation Department of a city in Wisconsin, continually received calls from individuals, clubs, and various organizations asking permission to do something in a park: to hold a fair, provide a service, perform a play, and so on. While giving permission for most activities presented no problem, there were other requests and favors he could not grant. For one thing, the department had a limited operating budget for equipment, material, and payroll. For another, some of the requests were not practical from a safety or health viewpoint or didn't meet the department's standards of good conduct.

Hal recognized that people strongly dislike the impersonal, cold refusal that leaves little room for doubt. So he always explained why he had to refuse a request. Over a period of time, Hal learned of alternative solutions to people's problems. When he had to say *no*, he made sure to mention such options. The citizens appreciated Hal's efforts to be helpful—in fact, many people often readily agreed that he was right in denying their request.

Being fair when you promote

The Problem

You are the supervisor of the nurses in the surgical section of a hospital on the north side of Chicago. Last year the board of directors decided to expand the hospital. Construction was started soon afterward and the job will be completed next month. With the addition of new facilities and beds, more nurses and supervisors will be needed. Naturally, there are a lot of questions being asked about where the new supervisors will come from. The head of the hospital was heard to say that he preferred to have the supervisors recruited by a personnel agency. However, some of the trustees have advised against this. Your superior has asked for your opinion on hiring supervisors from outside the hospital. But she has also asked you to review the qualifications of the people in your department and recommend those nurses who you think would make good supervisors. How should you answer her on hiring supervisors from the outside? If management decides to promote from within, how should it be handled?

The Solution

Obviously, if you feel that none of your people are qualified to be supervisors, management must either look elsewhere in the hospital for competent people or follow the outside-procurement procedure. However, promotion from within is generally recognized today as a cornerstone of good employment practice, and you should encourage the hospital to follow that practice whenever possible. When employees know that their company's policy is to promote from within whenever possible, some are motivated to be more loyal and to work hard for a better job.

A good way to foster internal promotion is to post information about the vacancy for at least five days to give all qualified full- and part-time personnel an equal opportunity to apply. The criteria for promotion usually include job performance, skills and competence, and attendance record. Date of employment may be the deciding factor for promotion only when all applicants for a job opening show equal qualifications. A recommendation for promotion should be discussed by the department manager and the personnel director for evaluation and approval. Transfer within the hospital should not affect seniority. Employees who are transferred or promoted and whose adjustment to the new job is not satisfactory during a trial period of 30 working days should be reinstated to their former jobs.

As for nurses who would make good supervisors, what about those people who have filled in for you in your absence? Assuming those people are qualified and did a good job, they should be a good choice. That is not to say they would accept the job if it were offered them. Don't be surprised if you have to "sell" an individual on the prospect of a supervisory position. Not everyone wants the responsibility that goes with a better job.

How One Supervisor Counseled Unpromotable Employees

The retail food industry generally is a low-profit one, and some supermarkets are not able to pay their employees well in comparison to other organizations. Henry M., supervisor of the cashiers and checkout people in a supermarket in Chicago, continually faces employees' requests for wage increases and promotions that will enable them to earn more money. Unfortunately, there weren't many higher positions to which his people could be promoted. Whenever an infrequent opening occurred, Henry took the time to explain to employees why they hadn't been promoted.

First he described the full responsibilities of the opening. Then he told the disappointed person which particular skills or abilities he or she was lacking, and he provided facts to support what he said. Henry then explained how the candidate chosen came closest to meeting the needs of the job. Henry let the person know that he or she had been seriously considered for the job, that his or her contribution to the company over the years was recognized and appreciated, and that the person was well liked. He added that many co-workers expected the applicant to get the job. Lastly, Henry helped the person to prepare for the future. He found out what that person wanted and he discussed the steps necessary to achieve those goals. By talking with a department member about a promotion that didn't materialize, Henry treated the person with the respect he or she deserved.

14

Time and How to Manage It

The way you manage your time determines how successful you are and also has an effect on your health and happiness. There is no such thing as "not enough time." If you feel that you are too busy to be efficient, look at the people who are busier than you and still get more accomplished. The same amount of time is available to all of us—some people just use their time better.

Wasting time is an expensive habit, but one that can be broken. As a supervisor, you should do your best to minimize the time wasted by people in your department. Saving time cuts costs. People on the job should help their company by giving it the time they're being paid for. A few minutes devoted to planning your day and organizing your work can increase your efficiency as well as your productivity. Adopting timesaving habits is the way to make time work for you and those you supervise.

Time and how to manage it when you must decide what to do first

The Problem

You supervise the designers in a small plant in Buffalo, New York, that manufactures electrical appliances. You have a lot of responsibilities, sometimes more than you think you should have. You often start the day with many jobs to do, and not enough people to do them. During the day you receive requests for design work from several departments and your boss frequently asks you to conduct special studies. In addition, you have some ideas of your own that you would like to see tried. There never seems to be a letup in the work for your department, yet management will not give you any more people and will not allow people to work overtime except on rare occasions. How do you decide which jobs to do first? How can you make the best use of your department's time and your own?

The Solution

Take a few minutes each morning to figure out the best way to make the most of the time available to your department. As for deciding what *you* should do first, start with the job that is most on your mind. Your effectiveness and efficiency are diminished when you are tense or worried, so it's a good idea to relieve such feelings as soon as you can. When you are less anxious you will be able to do a better job on your other tasks. For example, you may be uptight about having to reprimand someone in your department. After you have handled this matter you will be better able to put your mind on other work.

In deciding what to do next, give priority to a job that someone has requested that you handle quickly. Of course, first complete work that your boss has requested, then concentrate on jobs that other departments have asked for. The work that needs to be done to satisfy only yourself should receive the lowest priority.

The supervisor who plans his or her work daily takes a big step toward being more efficient. Being more efficient means saving time. You and the people you supervise will get more accomplished and the problem of what to do first won't loom quite as large. Too many supervisors start their day by doing what first comes to their attention or what they suddenly remember was not handled the day before. By doing whatever comes up first, they often put the cart before the horse. Doing important things first is a sign of maturity and experience.

How a Supervisor Saved Time on Routine Jobs

Helen F., supervisor of the typists and clerks in a life insurance company in Canton, Ohio, assigned many routine jobs every day. She found that when she had to handle many of the jobs on the spur of the moment she was tense and fatigued at the end of the day and hadn't accomplished everything that she had hoped to.

In trying to get her work done faster and more efficiently, she found that there are two ways to take care of routine jobs quickly. First, she got into the habit of doing the same job at the same time each day. She learned that she fit into the swing of the task much faster and didn't overlook some part of it. Because habit took over, she went through the motions automatically. Second, she concentrated on doing one thing at a time. She saw that jumping back and forth on jobs delayed her because she needed "review" time on each occasion to pick up where she had left off.

You can benefit from the experience of Helen. Do most of your routine work at the same time each day, and try to finish one job before you start another. Remember this when you are assigning work to others. They'll be much more efficient.

Time and how to manage it when you must deal with slow starters

The Problem

Vicky N., supervisor of the copywriters at an advertising firm in New York, has several specialists working for her. These professionals prepare copy for the firm's clients in the city. Many of the requests for copy come to the firm with a 24-hour deadline, thus putting pressure on the writers to get their work out quickly.

Although the writers have been taught to constantly "think advertising" and to draw on their life experiences and understanding of what motivates people, they often are not easily motivated themselves. As a result, Vicky must push them to be creative and to get the job done. She has the most difficulty in doing this at the beginning of the day, because many of the writers are slow starters. They can't seem to break the habit of having another cigarette or cup of coffee before getting to work. What should Vicky do to get people to "dig in" earlier? Why are some people difficult to motivate early in the morning?

The Solution

Vicky's slow starters waste much valuable time. She should try to give them new assignments late in the afternoon. They will then pick up a partially completed job in the morning; it's much easier to get going on such work than it is to tackle a new job. Fiction writers frequently use this strategy to maintain momentum from one day to the next. They will leave a scene or conversation between characters incomplete when they stop writing at the end of the day. Since they already know how to finish that section, it is easier to sit down and begin working on the next day.

Another way that Vicky can get her slow starters going is to schedule their appointments with clients as early as possible in the day. She can also hold staff meetings the first thing in the morning. By the time those meetings are finished, her people should be alert and in a better frame of mind for working.

Sociologists have classified people into "night" persons and "day" persons. The former are at their best late in the day and into the night; the latter, early in the day. Slow starters are quite frequently night people. If you are a day person, you must be patient with your nocturnal counterpart, who is often at a disadvantage professionally in a society geared to early-starting business operations.

How Another Supervisor Handled Slow Starters

Each morning in the office of an automobile insurance company in Wheeling, West Virginia, supervisor P. Bailey personally delivers a report to his underwriters. He does this promptly at 9:00, the starting time for the office. Bailey goes through this routine for several reasons. It gives him an opportunity to greet his people, exchange a few words on mutual interests with them, and make some comments on the priority of jobs for the day. His appearance breaks up the "bull sessions" that eat up company time and prompts slow-starting individuals to begin work.

Small groups of idlers or slow starters will usually disperse if you ask for the help of one member on some matter—help that requires the person to leave with you to go to his or her workplace, or yours. Removing one member of a group often gets the message across to the others that they should be getting their work done.

Time and how to manage it when it is wasted by excessive socializing

The Problem

The business machine operators whom you supervise at a bank in Philadelphia are friendly and social people. Many of them are young and single, and the jobs they hold are their first ones. Because they are unaccustomed to spending eight hours a day on the job, they waste much of their time; their inexperience also accounts for their being unproductive. A large share of the time wasted by these people can be attributed to late starts, early quits, long lunch times, and excessive socializing.

Although the bank has issued a "Rules for Employees" booklet that covers these matters, it is generally ignored. A few days ago your boss suggested that you keep your people busy more of the time. He said that when he went by the department last week, only a few machines were running. What should you do to limit the time wasted by your people? What should you say to them?

The Solution

Every employee of every company spends some time on the job socializing. Conversation among your people is vital to their morale and enthusiasm and promotes teamwork. (That's not true of late starts and early quits, which *must* be kept under control.) When it is obvious that lengthy and frequent conversations or get-togethers are exclusively social events, you should take action to limit them. You must curb the repeated and constant abuse of such a privilege, which eats up productive company time.

Begin by concentrating on the worst offenders. If you can get them in line, others will likely follow suit. Talk to the late arrivers personally and privately, pointing out the starting time in the office. Tell them that you expect them to be ready to work at that time, not to simply arrive then. Handle the early quitters similarly; mention that they are being paid for eight hours of work a day and they are expected to devote that time to the company. Be sure, of course, that *you* put in a full day's work—that you are always on the job early and that you are still there when your people leave.

A second step you should take is to talk to all of your people in a group meeting. It is not necessary to single out the worst offenders; everyone knows who goofs off and spends the least time on the job.

Group discussions demonstrate to employees that management recognizes the problem and is trying to do something about it, and such discussions may prompt employees to put pressure on the guilty individuals. This usually happens in organizations where wages are based on the team or group output. If some workers in a group begin to slip, the others bring them back in line.

Admonishment about wasting time has more of an impact when you talk to people at the moment they are guilty of the offense. To the person who takes a lot of personal time off, make comments such as, "I've missed you. Is everything all right?" or "You've been gone a long time. Are you feeling ill?" One or two remarks of that nature may be enough to bring an end to wasting time away from the job.

With habitual offenders, you may need to take disciplinary action. Be sure that such people are warned beforehand. Simply dock them for an amount of time equal to that wasted.

How Another Supervisor Curbed Time Wasters

Ron T., supervisor of the production department of a chemicals company in Dow, Michigan, realized that many of the goals that management set for the department required close coordination of various processes under his control. He was also aware that the production schedule demanded that his people be efficient and not waste time. Management thought highly of Ron because he recognized his responsibilities in both of these areas.

Ron was successful as a supervisor because he learned that his presence was often all that was needed to keep his people on the job and doing good work. By frequently visiting the work areas, he kept up to date on job progress, quickly got a jump on problems that arose with the work, and showed an interest in the employees. He didn't always discuss the job when he came to their work areas because he found it better to talk to people about their interests while he simply observed what was going on. With this approach, his people didn't resent his presence or feel that he was oversupervising them. But because they never knew when he would appear, workers didn't overextend their break or lunch periods and limited their socializing.

If you sit in your office much of the time, you can't stay on top of the job and be sure that your people are getting out the work. A good supervisor must be available without appearing to look over workers' shoulders.

Time and how to manage it when interruptions affect your efficiency

The Problem

As supervisor in the specifications department of a steel company in Gary, Indiana, you have ten writers and draftsmen working for you. Product specifications change frequently since the company promotes customized orders and will accept any order regardless of its size. In addition, the research and development departments actively pursue test programs for new applications. What this all amounts to is a lot of work passing through your hands, making for hectic, stressful days. Yet, at the end of a day when you look back at what you accomplished, you realize that you were not very efficient.

Your typical day is a series of interruptions: Supervisors of other departments frequently drop in your office to follow up on their work requests, a writer needs help on wording, a draftsman questions a design, and your boss wants to discuss some changes that have been proposed. You receive more phone calls than any other supervisor in the company. What should you do about these interruptions, which are affecting your efficiency? Is there a way to eliminate them?

The Solution

Interruptions destroy blocks of time, and that hurts your productivity. You can rarely pick up a job where you left off; usually, you must back up a bit. If you have numerous interruptions, you may find yourself doing certain parts of a job two, three, or four times.

The types of interruptions you should control are those that are easily deferred or completely avoidable. You must start saying *no* to the question, "Do you have a minute?" If you have an office door, close it when you are busy and don't want your train of thought interrupted. Also, avoid eye contact with people passing by. In today's society, eye contact, once established, makes interruption compulsory.

If you are continually interrupted by certain supervisors, schedule regular meetings with those people. They will soon learn that they can handle their business with you at the meeting rather than interrupt you at other times. Avoiding interruptions by your writers and draftsmen can be minimized if you visit them at your convenience. Once they know that you periodically will come by, they will hold their questions until that time. As a supervisor, you should be following up with your people on a regular basis anyway. As for interruptions by your boss, there isn't much you can or should do to prevent them. You don't want to give the impression that you've lost enthusiasm for the job or are not willing to accept challenges.

Shut out telephone interruptions by having the person who takes your calls handle messages when you are busy. If you handle your own calls, let frequent callers know when the best time for you is.

When inevitable interruptions do occur, give the interruption your full attention. Irritation and preoccupation are harmful to communication during an interruption because they lead to poor human relations. Therefore, unless you can give the interruption your full attention, don't let it occur. Also, do your best to take control of an interruption so that you can keep it short.

What Another Supervisor Did About Interruptions

Soon after taking the job of supervisor of the quality control clerks in an electrical appliances firm in West Allis, Wisconsin, Becky W. saw that she would be frequently interrupted. Because of the large volume of detailed records that she was responsible for, she decided to do her best to keep interruptions short. Becky was fairly successful in doing this by maintaining an attitude of being interrupted when it happened. She continually gave the impression of being very busy by leaning forward in her chair and keeping a pencil in her hand. By placing the only chair in a far corner away from her desk, she made it less appealing for an interrupter to get seated in her office. And she shortened conversations by rising from her own seat when she felt a communication could be ended.

Any person who wants to minimize or prevent interruptions can learn the subtle body communication that provides this message. If you have not already done so, you should give it a try. The skill will frequently come in handy.

Time and how to manage it when you are too busy to be efficient

The Problem

You are the supervisor of the procedures and specifications department for a manufacturing company whose headquarters is in New Jersey. The company has several plants located throughout the country and offers a broad product line. Because product styles change continually, the number of forms, drawings, and specifications that pass through your department is very large. Although 12 people work for you, there are many times when the accumulation of orders puts the department about two weeks behind in processing the paperwork and sending it on to management for approval. You never seem to have enough time to get caught up, and you sense that the backlog is going to increase rather than diminish. What can you do to better manage your time and get more done? Is there something you can do to make your people more productive?

The Solution

When you are too busy to be efficient, you should start looking at how you spend your time. Make sure you're not using time-consuming procedures just because you're used to doing jobs in a certain way or because the job has always been done that way. If you discover a time-saving way of performing a job, look for other areas where this same way could be used to advantage.

Determine if more planning and organizing will help. Often, a short time spent analyzing a situation and deciding what you need to do can save many hours of work. Write out procedures listing the steps to follow in doing a job so that good practices may be repeated. For some jobs, the procedures can serve as an explanation of the work, including instructions. Such documentation brings about order and uniformity and also comes in handy on jobs that are done infrequently and that people are prone to forget. Organize your files along the same lines. Place specifications, drawings, and other papers in the correct places, arranged in their best relation to each other and to your most efficient use.

Set priorities. Zero in on the most important work rather than skipping from one job to another. Do the big jobs and the tough jobs first, leaving the less important ones for later. Use odd moments, such as when you are waiting for someone, to read reports, letters, and the like.

People who think they are too busy to be efficient should realize that it isn't what they start but what they finish that counts. You must constantly go forward after you start, following one action with the next logical one if you expect to do something properly and efficiently. Lack of time is not a problem—it's only an excuse.

How Another Supervisor Handled Time More Efficiently

Claire R., supervisor of office services at a power facility in Niagara Falls, was on the job for only a few months when she realized that she needed to organize her department and establish new work techniques. Too much of her own and her subordinates' time was being wasted. In order to look for answers, she decided to determine how she was spending her time. For a week, therefore, she kept a record of what she did on the job, breaking each day down into 15-minute intervals. Then she listed her responsibilities and duties, taking into consideration her short- and long-term objectives. Referring to her time records, she identified the activities that were vital, sorting them out from the many trivial ones.

Claire found that she was spending up to three quarters of her time on trivial jobs that she could delegate to others or simply discontinue. Claire then established priorities and acted on them, doing the most important jobs first, not the easy, inconsequential ones. After a few weeks of conscientious efforts to make better use of her time, Claire found that she was accomplishing at least twice as much as she had earlier and that she was getting her important work done faster, besides. Just as important, she proved that if you want to, you can be more efficient—if you work at it.

15

Communication and How to Handle It

Supervisors get things done through others. To be effective and efficient, they must guide and lead people in directing what, how, and when something must be done. Their skill at communicating affects their success as supervisors.

There's a skill to communicating well, and you need to develop that skill in order to carry out your job responsibilities. In addition to instructing and giving orders, you must be able to promote and sell ideas, keep people informed, and provide the leadership expected of your position. The more proficient you are in communicating, the better you will be able to handle those responsibilities.

How do you become a skillful communicator? Aside from becoming knowledgeable about the language and its use, you develop an understanding of people and how they think. You learn the type and form of communication your listener prefers and you adopt it. In addition, you recognize the importance of timing so that you communicate at the right moment.

Communication and how to handle it when an employee won't listen to instructions

The Problem

Pete J., office machine repairman at the central offices of an insurance company in New York, was knowledgeable about repairing and maintaining the typewriters, copiers, and other similar machines in the offices. But the company was not entirely satisfied with Pete's performance on the job. On more than one occasion he had caused others to lose time in the offices by working on the wrong machine, by not making a specific adjustment as requested, and by failing to repair broken machines.

John S., his supervisor, was concerned about Pete's failures. When discussing them with Pete, he learned that Pete hadn't always followed instructions on job priorities either, preferring to handle easy repairs first. In some cases, Pete felt he knew better what should be done on a particular machine. In other instances, Pete had simply forgotten instructions because he had several machines to repair that day. How should John handle Pete? How can he get Pete to make fewer mistakes?

The Solution

John should realize that the problem he has to solve to make Pete a better worker mainly involves communication. John must do a better job of communicating with Pete. First, John should give Pete a written work order covering each job to be done. Second, he should take more time to discuss a job with Pete when he assigns it. When John senses misunderstanding or disagreement, he should ask Pete to repeat back to him what work is to be done.

In addition, Pete needs closer supervision. John should establish a work schedule for Pete each day and then periodically visit the job sites to see how he is doing. Following up will enable John to find out whether Pete is handling the most urgent jobs first and also whether the machine users are satisfied with the repairs made. John should adopt another technique to make Pete more receptive to instructions. He should make a point of discussing the unusual conditions Pete occasionally finds in his work. The early failure of a reliable machine part or a bad case of misalignment are examples. By talking about such matters, Pete will be less likely to proceed on questionable work without discussing it with John beforehand.

When you have an employee who doesn't follow your instructions, you must search and study your techniques to learn what makes you effective and what makes you ineffective. You must understand the person you are instructing and you must be knowledgeable about the problem or job to be handled. Finally, you must put all this knowledge together to make your approach suitable to the time, the place, the person, and the task.

How Another Supervisor Handled a Similar Problem

"Big Joe" W., supervisor of the planners for the management of a shopping center in Houston, Texas, learned that there were some days on the job when his people did not listen carefully to his instructions. Since this invariably resulted in work that had to be redone, Joe knew that he had to find the answer or answers to why this happened. In reviewing several incidents, he felt that the problem probably resulted from poor communicating on his part.

Joe was not at his best early in the morning and was often impatient with the workers. Fortunately, he recognized his weakness and was aware that impatience can hamper effective communication. When friction prevails, it is difficult to have a calm, comfortable exchange of ideas—and that is what communication is all about. So Joe began coming to his office a half-hour earlier each day. He found that he was in a better frame of mind when it was time to give people assignments.

Joe learned another thing. He found that he could more easily communicate what must be done if he prefaced his instructions with praise for what already had been done. The planners appreciate a good word on the work they have accomplished the day before, so Joe regularly offers such comments prior to handing out new assignments.

Communication and how to handle it when you must answer a complaint

The Problem

Mary J., a young, aggressive employee, works in the gas company offices where you are a supervisor. She is one of the best word processors you supervise, and came to your department from the office typing pool a few months ago. She asked for the transfer because, in her words, "my ability and speed in getting out the work weren't appreciated." In the last few weeks you've noticed that she doesn't hesitate to express her opinion on matters relating to her work. Although you've complimented her whenever she did unusually good work, she has complained when some of the work was difficult or she felt pushed to complete it quickly. Also, she constantly is comparing the amount of work you give her with what you give the other word processors. As she was leaving the office yesterday afternoon, she stopped at your desk to say, "Why don't you give more work to Jean and Cheryl? You're piling it all on me and that's not fair." Rather than ask her to stay late to discuss the matter, you suggested that you talk about it this morning. What should you say to Mary? How should you answer her complaint?

The Solution

Your suggestion that you discuss her complaint this morning was a good one because it gives you time to get facts and to learn what prompted the complaint. It's more important that you give her a good answer than a fast one. Look back at your recent assignments to Jean, Cheryl, and Mary. Determine if you've distributed the work fairly or if inadvertently you've given more to Mary because of her greater skill and speed. It is possible that Mary may be right in her claim.

By all means, answer Mary's complaint as promptly as you can, preferably as soon as she comes into the office. She may not do her work satisfactorily until you do so. Besides, you show your concern and sincerity when you take care of a complaint quickly. Complaints almost always are serious matters to those who make them—you must view Mary's in that light. Begin by telling her that you try to be fair in handing out the work, but you may have given her more because of your feeling that she did better, faster work than the other word processors. Say that you will be more careful about this in the future.

As an adjunct to your intention to get along with Mary and your other people by prompt and fair handling of their complaints, you should always search for the reason for a complaint. Does Mary feel she is underpaid? Is she perhaps jealous of Jean or Cheryl for any reason? Did she experience a setback recently? Your findings will guide you in how to help her get more satisfaction from her work. You already know that she doesn't feel appreciated. Give her more attention, commenting especially on her speed and accuracy.

Don't be disturbed about Mary's comment. In fact, be sure your other people know that they should talk to you whenever they are unhappy about a situation or a turn of events. Resentment not expressed leads to discontent, low morale, and even retaliation, all of which mean trouble. Sometimes an outside problem, one you have nothing to do with, is the cause of a complaint. Find the solution to it, if you can, and make a friend.

How Another Supervisor Avoided Complaints

Managers at an automobile assembly plant in Detroit recognized that they needed supervisors skilled in human relations in order to handle the labor problems that plagued the plant. An example of the type of individual they sought was Harry B., a man whose competence was demonstrated by the fact that his department had experienced the lowest number of complaints over the past year. Harry's boss had studied Harry's supervisory techniques and had shared them with the personnel department.

Harry made it easy for people in his department to come to him with problems and gripes by letting them know that he would not be defensive. He was always informal and tried to avoid red tape in working out solutions to problems. A quality he was especially admired for was his willingness to help a person put his or her feelings into words; Harry realized that if a person failed to complain because he or she was not articulate, that would just bottle up the person's discontent.

Harry always was patient with people regardless of how busy he was. He showed his patience by hearing a person out. He knew that a person couldn't do his or her best work if he or she was troubled. Although Harry tried to answer people promptly when they were unhappy or displeased, he never made hasty or biased decisions. When you consider all the attributes Harry possessed, it's understandable why management recognized him as one of the plant's best supervisors.

Communication and how to handle it when you promote modernization

The Problem

Kay S., office supervisor at a public accounting firm in New York City, aspires to a successful career in business. She did well in school, earned an M.B.A. degree, and is very knowledgeable about business procedures. In addition, she is familiar with up-to-date office equipment, business machines, and computer techniques. Shortly after being hired by the accounting firm, she saw that the company was using a lot of antiquated machines and procedures. Knowing that employees would be more productive and that fewer people might be needed if the office was modernized, Kay decided to try to sell management on the idea. How should she go about this? What steps should she take?

The Solution

Kay should realize that what she is going to propose has probably been thought of by management. Surely some executive has already recognized the need; in fact, the company may have a plan that will soon be adopted. So Kay's first step is to discuss the idea with her boss. She can save herself work as well as the embarrassment of appearing uninformed by asking about the company's plans before she does anything else.

Depending on where management stands and what it intends to do, Kay can decide how she can participate in the effort. Her boss may ask her for a letter promoting the idea with the intention of bringing up the subject at the next management meeting. Or he may ask her for specific recommendations for replacement of some equipment. Whatever, Kay should follow the chain of command in any proposal she makes on modernization.

Since thoughts of automation might create fear and bitterness among employees, damaging morale and causing a productivity decline, Kay should keep her efforts low-key at least until management is in a position to make some official announcements. Otherwise, rumors could fly. Management may be accused of unfair policies and may have to take some kind of action to reassure people that they will be considered in any action the company takes.

When you promote modernization or automation—or any major change, for that matter—you must consider people and how they will be involved. Problems concerning change are discussed in Chapter 18.

How Another Supervisor Communicated Modernization Plans

Paul W., supervisor of the mail room in a bank in Pittsburgh, recognized that management's plans to modernize his department would involve many changes in both the facilities and the employees. He knew that people would be concerned about the move and that many questions would be asked. With these things in mind, he suggested that management's plans and decisions be posted on the bulletin board rather than have the employees receive the news from him. Paul felt that this form of communicating would result in less doubt in the minds of all the department people on facts about the modernization as well as its timing. It would also be more credible relative to probable layoffs. Management bought Paul's idea. The announcement explained their intentions in detail and was presented in question and answer form. The questions were supplied by Paul, who best understood the employees' concern.

In business and industry today, the preferred way to transmit job-related information is through supervisors, because they are management in the minds of employees. As supervisors, the opportunity for them to give employees bits of information increases their stature. It also gives them a reason for frequent conversation with employees. Employees are more likely to feel that they are part of the organization when news is shared with them. Many times, however, when information filters down through several levels of management, false assumptions occur. In such circumstances, a more direct method of communicating information is necessary.

Communication and how to handle it when you want to get along better with the boss

The Problem

Harry V., supervisor in the drafting room of an engineering consulting firm in Toledo, Ohio, is a regimented and conservative person. As a former draftsman, he knows the importance of careful, detailed work and recognizes that documentation is necessary in order to have records that can be referred to later. Harry's communications with his boss, Tom B., are usually in written form. When he proposes a new procedure, reports on a project, or provides facts to support a theory, he always puts these things in writing. When he has only a short message to convey, he uses a memo.

Harry senses, however, that he doesn't get along with Tom as well as some of the other supervisors do. For one thing, he receives little feedback from him and Tom seems to ignore much of his work. Harry notices, too, that Tom visits the other supervisors more frequently than he comes to him. Although Harry realizes that he doesn't mix well with people, he hopes that this will not hold him back from advancing to a better job in the company. How can Harry better communicate with Tom? What should he do to improve his relations with him?

The Solution

Harry needs to begin communicating face to face with Tom. Harry should see that Tom prefers to communicate verbally—that is how he handles the other supervisors.

Harry must stir up interest in himself and his ideas if he expects to be promoted. Too often today, supervisors hope to move up to better jobs with their company but they do little to further their own cause. Although written reports may describe your accomplishments, bosses also look for personality, enthusiasm, and drive in their people, attributes that you display when you interact with people. Tom will never get to know Harry's capabilities if they don't periodically get together to discuss problems and courses of action.

It is better to speak to a person directly when you want to persuade or convince him or her. By observing how you are received, you know when to change your approach, whether to use soft or strong words, what points you need to emphasize, and what resistance you need to overcome. Such knowledge and insight is not possible with written communications.

Harry could further his cause also by sharing an outside interest with Tom. Professional organizations, clubs, civic groups, and plant committees are only a few such groups that welcome new members, especially when such members want to actively participate in the organization's functions. These functions could lead to conversation with Tom away from the office, enabling Tom to learn more about Harry and his interests. Such contacts can facilitate communication on the job.

How Another Supervisor Effectively Communicated with the Boss

W. Westman, supervisor of the traffic routers for a multiple product manufacturing firm in Connecticut, adopted a method of communicating with his boss based on what he saw of how other people handled him. For example, R. Stock, his boss, showed his aggressive let's-get-it-done nature by becoming impatient when conversations didn't move along quickly. Westman, therefore, made sure he knew what he wanted to say and how he would say it before he set foot in Stock's office.

Westman noticed, too, that Stock wrote a lot of memos and spent much time reading at his desk. This told Westman that his boss preferred to see proposals and suggestions in writing so that he could think about them. Stock maintained several files in his office and personally attended to them. This confirmed Westman's conclusion that his boss highly valued records that could be referred to from time to time; again a preference for the written word.

How you approach your boss can be just as critical as what you say or write to him or her. Study your boss to learn how he or she prefers to communicate. Then start doing it that way. You'll find that your communication problems will be minimized and you'll be better received besides.

Communication and how to handle it when you fill in for the boss

The Problem

W. Cottle is respected as a top-notch supervisor in the marketing department of a steel company whose main offices are in New York City. Although he has been with the company for only five years and has spent the last two as supervisor, he is in line for another promotion. To prepare him for a higher position with the company and to broaden his experience, management has decided to put him in charge of the department next month for a six- to eight-week period while his boss, R. Santo, has a surgical operation.

While Cottle is very pleased about being made a temporary manager and is not worried about handling the technical aspect of the job, he is concerned about getting along with his peers during Santo's absence, especially in communicating with them and giving them assignments. How should Cottle prepare for his temporary job as manager? What problems might he encounter in communicating with his peers and other individuals when he substitutes for the boss?

The Solution

Cottle should plan to spend much of his time with the boss the week before he fills in for him. Prior to that, however, he should begin to become familiar with his boss's duties and responsibilities. Undoubtedly, there are weekly and monthly reports that the boss issues; Cottle should become familiar with them. Santo may want Cottle to handle some of these prior to his absence so that he becomes accustomed to the procedure and knowledgeable about the content.

To pave the way for Cottle, Santo should issue a memo explaining that Cottle will be the acting manager during his absence. The memo should be sent to all individuals who interface with the department or Santo directly. Copies should also go to Cottle's peers.

Cottle should attempt to handle Santo's responsibilities as Santo would. He has the authority to do so and should have few if any problems communicating with his peers if they understand his position. He should try to keep them fully and correctly informed, recognizing that people on the job can't live in an informational vacuum. When there is an interruption in the flow of information, rumor and speculation quickly arise. Cottle should be careful about deciding that something *must* be kept secret. Secrets breed distrust—and they aren't kept for long. Usually when something has been definitely decided, it is wise to immediately announce it.

No matter whom you work for, you like to be in on things. You appreciate it when your boss takes you into his or her confidence and keeps you up to date about what's going on. When the boss fails to do so, you feel unimportant. The people who work for you feel the same way, and they feel it just as strongly as you do. Although Cottle should try to convey pertinent information, he should beware of passing along extraneous information. Such "flooding" confuses listeners as to just what's intended by the discussion.

How Another Supervisor Substituted for the Boss

Charles J. is the supervisor of a group of claims adjusters for an insurance company in Chicago. When he was recently asked to fill in for the boss while the boss traveled to Europe, Charles enthusiastically accepted. He realized that he should know more about his peers' preferences and work habits. Charles knew that a good personal relationship with these people would make his temporary job easier and would also forestall feelings of jealousy—feelings that could lead to misunderstanding or lack of cooperation.

Since Charles had a month to prepare, he began to occasionally chat with supervisors about their work and their responsibilities. He already knew something about most of the people from having attended meetings and other functions with them; he wanted to confirm his impressions and expand his knowledge. By showing an interest in them and by being friendly, Charles achieved several benefits: (1) He made it easy for them to accept assignments from him during the boss's absence; (2) he greatly increased his knowledge of his boss's responsibilities; (3) he learned how to communicate with each individual; and (4) he increased the probability of getting each person's cooperation.

It pays for a supervisor to be on good terms with his or her peers. You may someday be their boss, or one of them may be your boss.

16

Dispelling Rumors

Because one of the prime responsibilities of a supervisor is to keep his or her people informed, dealing with rumors becomes one of your duties. Few organizations today can claim that their people never start or spread rumors, although most managers wish this were true. If rumors are ignored they can cause hard feelings, embarrassment, and reduced productivity—therefore, they must be dealt with.

The best way to dispose of a rumor is to thoroughly investigate why it originated and to determine whether there is any truth to the matter. Be sure to tell your department what you are doing and assure people that you will inform them of what you learn. Talk to your boss about the rumor first, then consult other authorities if necessary.

You dispel rumors by giving people the facts. If there is no truth to a rumor, say so. If you have no information, tell them that. Above all, ask your workers to never repeat a rumor. As a supervisor, you must show people that you intend to do everything possible to keep them fully informed.

Dispelling rumors concerning your department

The Problem

Lisa R., a clerk in the general offices of a food company in Minnesota, is a compulsive talker. As one of her duties, she delivers reports, mail, memos, and so on to various offices, a task that takes her two to three times longer than it should because she has a conversation with at least one person at each office. She arranges to do her filing at the same time as a clerk from another department so that they can talk with each other.

However, there's another related problem you're having with Lisa. She seems to delight in originating and spreading rumors—you can find no other source of the gossip and rumors that periodically circulate through the company about your department. According to the latest rumor now making the rounds, there will soon be a 10 percent reduction in personnel in your department. What should you do about such rumors? Should you ask Lisa if she has been talking to people about this rumor?

The Solution

In every organization, employees occasionally spread rumors about a change they have heard is about to take place. While there may be no way you can completely prevent such talk, there is a way to control it. You can put a damper on rumors by keeping people informed. Rumors flourish most when employees don't have knowledge or information about matters that concern them. A rumor won't get started or grow if the facts are known.

Keep people informed about changes before they occur. If a new procedure is being considered by management or a personnel change is to be made, tell people about it quickly before they have an opportunity to guess or try to figure out what is going to happen. Once a rumor starts, it's tough to stop it. Recognize that whatever you say carries weight, and facts are your best ammunition.

In the present situation, assuming there is no truth to the rumor of a layoff, tell your people that the department needs to reduce its costs, and that laying off employees was considered as it always is in such situations. But emphasize that the company does this only as a last resort. Explain that other ways to cut costs always exist and some have been adopted.

Supervisors must remember that what they say to one employee will reach the ears of others. They must be careful to avoid making comments that are easily misconstrued. Again, the best way to eliminate rumors is to keep employees informed. A rumor won't get started when the truth is known.

Step up your efforts to make Lisa more efficient and to limit her conversations on matters other than business. Tell her that she wastes too much time talking and as a result is slow about her deliveries and her filing. It would not be proper to confront her about originating or spreading rumors—you have no proof of this. But you can tell her that *no one* should repeat a rumor. You can't stop people from talking about department activities, and many people simply don't try to separate rumor from fact—both are something to talk about. But you can tell them to stop making fact out of rumor.

How Another Supervisor Squelched Rumors

Doug K., supervisor of the draftsmen and designers in an aircraft manufacturing plant in Los Angeles, had worked as a design specialist for three years before being promoted to supervisor. During those years he and his family felt very insecure because of the uncertainty of the company's procurement of orders. Doug was never sure from month to month whether he would have a job, because commercial airline orders were often indefinite and occasionally cancelled. In addition, the aircraft company was frequently bidding on government contracts of various types. Since many contracts called for delivery within a limited time period, the number of people employed by the company fluctuated considerably from year to year. Under such a situation, rumors were wild and frequent. Employees often reached false conclusions about orders when they overheard bits of managers' conversations.

Shortly after becoming supervisor, Doug made a crusade of trying to reduce the number of rumors that passed through his department. He appealed to his boss for information that he could pass along every Friday at a staff meeting. Doug prepared a running report that listed the open orders the company currently was handling, contracts on which the company was bidding, and contracts that the company had been recently awarded. Although this weekly report didn't completely eliminate rumors, it did serve to drastically reduce their number as well as their scope. Employees knew they would have the facts on Friday and they would not have to guess whether what they'd heard had any truth to it.

Dispelling rumors about you

The Problem

Ever since you became supervisor in the communications department of your company, an adhesives manufacturing firm in St. Paul, Minnesota, you've had to work hard to show people that you're capable and deserving of the job. It seems that many people feel that a woman should not be supervising a group that is predominantly male. After people get to know you and see how you handle the job, they often confess that they were mistaken in thinking that the job would be too difficult for you.

In another area you have not been as fortunate. During the past few weeks people have been spreading rumors about you, and what they have been saying has not been favorable. One of the rumors is that you have been socializing with one of the married bosses. That upsets you, perhaps more than it should. You wish that whoever is spreading those lies would stop; you sense that some people believe a part if not all of them. What should you do about the rumors? Is there any way you can stop them?

The Solution

Few situations can be more disturbing than discovering that someone is telling lies about you. You may get the feeling that you are fighting an unknown person, yet you've got to do something to defend yourself and protect your reputation. It's normal that you should want to fight back as hard as you can by telling everybody the facts. You'd also like to know who started the stories and why he or she did so. Unfortunately, however, drastic or aggressive action on your part will not do much good. People may listen to you defending yourself, wonder why you are so upset, and then conclude from your concern that there must be some truth to the rumors. It is better that you treat the whole matter calmly and show only minor interest. Talk to those people who are most affected by the rumors and tell them your side. You needn't try to explain to everyone. Simply tell the truth and let it go at that. It's very likely that the whole matter will end there with you having the last word. If you are successful, people will admire you for your effectiveness and strength.

You may not want the matter to rest there, however. You may want to know who might have benefited from the rumor. While you probably will not be able to learn who was behind or started the rumor, the person who could benefit is the one to watch. If a person is willing to lie to tear you down, he or she may do something desperate later.

Rumors and gossip exist wherever people get together. Stories you hear about other people are similar to those being told about you. Some people delight in this activity, considering it fun. But when they are spurred by ulterior motives, that's a different matter. If you don't fight it, you risk being considered guilty or stupid or both. You may be upset to learn that people are talking about you, but it is even worse not to know what is being said. Your best defense is to be alert and keep your eyes and ears open.

How Another Supervisor Handled Rumors
About Himself

Rumors are likely to be popular in a plant that is strongly unionized and is experiencing difficulties with employees over contract matters such as work jurisdiction. Rudy T., supervisor of the mechanics in an automotive plant in Hudson, Ohio, found that to be the case. A few of the radical members of the union occasionally resorted to spreading rumors about management people, including supervisors, as a way of retaliating for what they considered unfair treatment. Nevertheless, Rudy learned how to contend with such tactics.

Whenever a rumor concerned him personally, Rudy immediately told his boss what he'd heard and asked if there was any truth to the matter. He knew that his boss would know and would level with him. After being assured that what he'd heard was simply rumor, Rudy quickly cleared himself with his close associates, giving them the facts. He found that this was the best way to handle rumors and to prevent them from hurting himself or others.

Dispelling rumors that hinder productivity

The Problem

Esther G., supervisor of the word processors and key punchers at an insurance office in Philadelphia, was proud of her group of people. Although ranging in age from 22 to 58, they generally got along well together and kept up with their work. Esther knew that the people in the claims department weren't nearly so compatible. A grapevine system of communication had developed there sometime in the past and now flourished. It was commonly known that if you wanted to hear the latest rumor, you should talk to one of two people in that department. Esther felt fortunate that rumors about her department were relatively rare.

Yesterday the situation changed. Esther noticed that during the coffee break, a woman from the claims department had visited with one of the word processors. Shortly afterward, several people in her department stopped working to talk among themselves. When Esther approached they reluctantly returned to their desks. A similar situation arose in the afternoon, and then Esther decided to intervene. One of the office workers told Esther they had heard that the company was going to ask employees to take pay cuts to offset recent losses. What should Esther do? The rumor had already caused workers to lose productive time, and it would probably result in more time being lost.

The Solution

If ignored, rumors can destroy morale and productivity. Esther has already seen how people left their work to talk about simple hearsay. Before Esther can fight a rumor, she has to know what she's up against. She should ask her workers exactly what they've heard and where. Then she should tell them she'll investigate the matter and get back to them as soon as possible.

Esther should first talk to her boss to learn if there is any truth to the matter. If there is, she should find out if a statement can be issued immediately. Once she learns what she can say, she should call her people together and give them the facts. If there is no truth to the rumor, that is what they should be told. If she can't tell them anything, she should tell them *that*. At the same time, she may be able to tell them what is *not* true. Most important is that she demonstrate her concern and her interest in their welfare. She will be respected for it.

Rumors should never be permitted to interfere with getting the work out. If you find yourself in a situation similar to Esther's, tell your people to go ahead with their work as if they had not heard the rumor. Caution them against further speculation until you get the facts.

Some people spread rumors because they relish the thrill of being avidly listened to as they pass out the latest "news." Any bit of conversation they overhear, anything they've seen in a letter, or anything they've assumed gives them an opportunity to command an attentive audience. Truth is secondary. But rumors are an expensive nuisance that must be quelled.

How Another Supervisor Handled Rumors in His Department

Early in his career, Harmon B., supervisor in a trucking terminal in Cleveland, Ohio, learned that rumors can hurt. He knew several drivers and hand truckers who had acted foolishly or prematurely on a rumor that had spread through the terminal. In some cases, the person was embarrassed in front of his or her peers in addition to suffering a financial loss. In others, the employee's productivity fell until the truth came out. In all cases, rumors never helped the employees or the company.

Harmon was determined to do all he could to stop the gossip and idle talk in his department. He believed that rumors are usually an indication that communication between management and employees is inadequate. Whenever he heard or learned of a rumor, he immediately used official company communications, such as memos or bulletin-board notices, to give his people the facts. To each notice he added a note to discourage the people who spread rumors. The note read, "What can *you* do about rumors? The most important thing is to not pass them on. Pause and think about it when you are tempted. You really have nothing to gain, but you could hurt someone. Would you want to do that?"

17

Overcoming Procrastination

The biggest roadblock to achieving goals is procrastination. People procrastinate most often when they have an unpleasant or difficult job to do. Since everyone procrastinates to some degree, we must learn how to contend with it if we are to be efficient and productive. Supervisors can help themselves by knowing what to do when their boss or a fellow supervisor falls victim to it.

There are many ways you can procrastinate, and perhaps just as many ways you can overcome it. You won't defer action nearly as much if you develop a positive, optimistic viewpoint toward jobs, work, and duties. Realize that situations usually are not as bad as they may seem. Decide early on that you cannot continue to put off something indefinitely.

A reward awaits those of us who do not permit ourselves to procrastinate. When you finish a job that you would have liked to put off, you'll get a bit more satisfaction than you do from getting other jobs done (maybe you'll call it relief).

Overcoming procrastination when your boss is guilty of it

The Problem

Elaine T. is a supervisor in the data processing group in the offices of an oil company in New York City. The company is an old-line organization whose building, offices, and equipment have not changed in more than 20 years—except for the addition of some new office machines and the introduction of a computer system. Lighting is inadequate and the lack of air conditioning contributes to the discomfort of employees on hot summer days. Since the facilities, walls, and floors are in poor condition, keeping the area neat and clean is difficult.

The people working for Elaine began complaining to her about working conditions more than a year ago. She agrees with them and has talked to her boss, Paula K., several times about the need to modernize the office. Each time she brings up the subject, Paula agrees that something should be done, but she doesn't act. Lately, Paula said she was going to send her boss a letter pointing out the poor conditions and asking that improvements be made. But when Elaine brought up the subject again today, Paula said that she had been too busy and would get to it next week. Is there anything Elaine can do to get Paula to act on this matter? What reason or reasons could Paula have for procrastinating?

The Solution

Elaine should ask for Paula's permission to write the letter, adding that she and Paula can put it in final form before it is sent off. This request should bring the matter to a head, one way or another. Paula is procrastinating for one or more reasons: She is not entirely convinced that modernization is necessary at this time; she knows that management will not approve; or she feels that she would be overstepping her bounds. But the truth should now come out, so the problem can become clear to Elaine.

Many bosses have devised defense strategies to avoid taking action or making a decision. One of their favorite dodges is to claim that the timing isn't right. Another is to create a smokescreen as a diversionary tactic. A third is to simply refer to precedent as a reason for not doing something.

If you want to help a boss who is procrastinating, you must learn why he or she has been putting off a job that should be done. Admittedly, this is not always easy to do. When you bring up the subject, try not to do all the talking. A period of silence during the discussion may prompt a confession, after which you can offer help appropriate to the circumstances. If the boss resorts to a dodge, accept if for the moment. After a while, ask the boss if his or her reason is the same. That is about as far as you can go.

How Another Supervisor Handled a Boss Who Procrastinated

Beverly P., supervisor of the nurses in the maternity ward of a hospital in Topeka, Kansas, reported to the floor superintendent, Helen F., a woman in her fifties who had been working in the nursing profession for more than 30 years. Beverly was aggressive, enthusiastic, and genuinely liked people. She was highly sympathetic to the plight of the nurses on her ward, who were presently working long hours and seven days a week. But Beverly sensed that Helen didn't share her feelings in this matter.

When the board of directors approved the ward's request to hire two new nurses, Beverly was very pleased. The extra people would allow her to institute a rotation plan to give each of the nurses a day off every ten days. But Helen did not immediately begin to interview people for the new jobs. Although Beverly didn't understand Helen's delay, she felt that the situation was serious enough for her to try to overcome Helen's procrastination. She, therefore, informed all her people of the board's action and told them that she hoped the new nurses would soon be on the job. She also "gave permission" for two of the nurses to tell Helen how pleased they were that they would soon not have to work every day. Within two weeks, the nurses were on a rotational work system based on the two additions.

If you can subtly put pressure on someone who is procrastinating, you may be able to actually help the person to handle the matter. The more people who know a person is procrastinating, the greater the pressure on the person to overcome it. Of course, you must be very diplomatic in what you say or do when you fight procrastination in this manner. You do not want to be considered a judge, especially if the procrastinating person is sensitive to criticism.

Overcoming procrastination when you are guilty of it

The Problem

You are the supervisor in the research and development department for a paint company in Cleveland, Ohio. In addition to providing direction and guidance to chemists and technicians, you are responsible for periodically updating the department's files, testing new materials, diagnosing the cause of paint failures, and testing competitive products.

While your job keeps you busy and is challenging as well as interesting, you don't enjoy the reporting and documenting work that you are required to do. You often find yourself putting off writing test and progress reports and reporting failure analyses. You realize that you are procrastinating and you recognize that you are not helping yourself when you must admit to your boss that you have not completed an important part of your work. What can you do to overcome your problem? What makes you procrastinate?

The Solution

You most frequently succumb to procrastination when you are faced with an unpleasant task or a difficult decision. Often a job seems more unpleasant when you are not convinced of the need for doing it.

The best way to overcome procrastination is to tackle the unpleasant or difficult jobs when you are at your best—when your mind and body are fresh. Then go after the jobs with determination until you get them done. Recognizing that you are procrastinating is a prerequisite to overcoming it. Sometimes you must carefully analyze and think over an issue to make a good decision. You must be sure you have all the relevant information, including others' opinions, before making a move. If a decision is important, remember that the participation of other people can act as a spur to making the decision.

Another way to overcome procrastination is to promise someone you'll handle the matter within a specified time. When you have thus committed yourself, it is very difficult not to carry out your promise— your conscience just won't let you put the job off if you know someone is waiting for you to act.

If you are deferring several duties or jobs, decide that you'll handle the most urgent one first and then do one a day until they are wiped out. With this approach, you'll get a feeling of relief as well as satisfaction at each completion. Once you partially beat procrastination, it is much easier to overcome it in the future. Moreover, you will have demonstrated to yourself that you are strong-willed and capable of doing what must be done.

How Another Supervisor Avoided Procrastinating

Ned B., supervisor of the programmers in an insurance office in Boston, Massachusetts, was determined to rise to a high position in the company. He had learned self-discipline when getting his education and had always been able to use time efficiently. In addition, he was usually successful in motivating people on the job.

Ned found that the best way to overcome procrastination was to set deadlines for achieving goals. He had always done this with his personal affairs, so it was natural for him to carry out his supervisory responsibilities in the same way. He helped those he supervised to commit their goals to writing, making them specific and clearly measurable. He also insisted that a timetable be established for each project so that there would be no misunderstanding. Under these conditions, procrastination was seldom a problem in his department.

To be an effective supervisor, you must first be able to manage yourself. The most effective way of managing yourself is through planning—by establishing personal goals and setting deadlines for their accomplishment. When you have set goals for yourself you learn not to procrastinate. You also manage your time better and maintain good self-discipline.

Overcoming procrastination when a peer is guilty of it

The Problem

One of the subjects your boss discussed last week in his meeting with you and the other engineering department supervisors concerned the installation of a new machine in a division of your plant. The production department does not intend to operate this machine for at least three weeks, so the engineering department has that much time to install the equipment and try it out.

You are the supervisor of the electricians, who will finish the project after the mechanics do their portion of the job. However, you have already encountered a problem with the project. The supervisor of the mechanics, Bill G., has been assigning his people work other than on the new machine, work which you know is not of high priority. Three days ago you asked him if he would start the project, saying that you would like to begin the circuits and supply line. You told him also that the total electrical work would require at least two weeks of concentrated effort by your department. He replied that he would put his people on the job immediately—but he failed to do so. What should you do? Should you mention Bill's procrastination to your mutual boss?

The Solution

The sooner you sit down with Bill to again discuss the new machine installation, the better. Overcoming procrastination is often difficult—you may need to talk to Bill and remind him of the situation once more before he responds. First, explain that you can't do most of the work until *after* his mechanics have completed theirs. People who procrastinate will sometimes ask, "What's the hurry? You could have started your part of the job and you haven't." There's always the possibility, too, that your boss gave Bill orders *not* to start the job until some other work was done, and Bill failed to tell you this.

Ask Bill if there's some way you could help him with his portion of the job, such as by ordering or picking up material. Such an offer from you will remind him of his delinquency and may even be enough to get him moving. Or offer to help with the planning and layout. If your company has no union work jurisdictions, you can suggest that some of your people start the job under his supervision.

You would probably not remain on good terms with Bill if you mentioned his procrastination to your boss—it's better that you rely on your persuasive power to get Bill going. Besides, your boss, if he is on top of his job, may soon ask Bill about the status of the project himself.

You can commiserate with a fellow supervisor about the difficulty of overcoming procrastination but you will do more good by instead helping the person to get started, since that is the true hurdle. The solution is often contained in the approach: more often than not, once a problem is faced, it can be cut down to size and handled promptly.

How Another Supervisor Handled
Her Peer's Procrastination

Denise K., supervisor of office operations at a mail-order house in Maine, was one of two such persons the company employed. The two supervisors were very capable and skilled in their work and often helped each other when the workload became unbalanced. Denise, however, had a personal quality that Alexander lacked. In addition to being highly perceptive of people's feelings, she also possessed a high degree of empathy. Both of these human traits enabled her to occasionally come to Alexander's aid.

Alexander put off doing some of his work, particularly when it came to handling human relations problems. As a result, his department was undisciplined. He failed to dispose of many routine personnel problems, even when reminded by his superior that they were his responsibility. Whenever Denise perceived or heard of a "difficult" situation in Alexander's department, she immediately visited him and worked the problem into their conversation. By motivation and encouragement she provided the support Alexander needed to promptly alleviate a situation or mete out discipline.

18

Overcoming Resistance to Change

In business and industry today, new products, processes, procedures, regulations, and job positions constantly bring about change. Change is inevitable, yet many people resist it, especially on the job. Supervisors must do all they can to get their people to expect, understand, and prepare for change. The more they can do along these lines, the less resistance they will encounter.

It's natural to fear change, and most of us do, for one reason or another. Change is welcomed only when people demand it to relieve themselves of a burden or a discomfort. When things change, people don't know what to expect—even small alterations disturb routines and habits, causing worry and stress.

It's easier to overcome resistance if you can get people involved with changes before making them. You must, of course, be sure a modification is worthwhile and beneficial, and you should keep it as simple as possible. Change is more acceptable also if it is made without a lot of fanfare and publicity.

Lastly, give people time to live with and adjust to a change. Resistance won't disappear immediately.

Overcoming resistance to change exhibited by employees

The Problem

Wayne B., your senior accountant, has been with the company for 32 years. Your manufacturing firm in Racine, Wisconsin, has made a lot of changes in its bookkeeping and accounting procedures during that time, including adopting a comprehensive computer data base and a sophisticated information retrieval system. But Wayne is a stubborn person and resists new procedures and methods in the office. It is apparent that he feels much more secure with the ledgers and files he has been accustomed to working with.

In some cases, his unwillingness to change has caused him to criticize the new methods to fellow accountants by pointing out any and all weaknesses that he thinks exists. But as far as you can see, he has not succeeded in changing the thinking of his peers. Should you clamp down and tell him to stop finding fault with the new system before others begin believing him? How should you swing him over to accept the new methods?

The Solution

It would not be wise for you to overtly pressure Wayne to stop fighting change. More likely than not, this would only focus sympathy on him. It's better to simply listen to him, tell him you understand how he feels, and draw him out to learn his true concerns. Then you can allay his fears and assure him that the new ways are best for the company. For the time being, let him get involved in them at his own pace.

Look back to see how Wayne was introduced to the new methods. Were his ideas and thoughts solicited? Did he participate in some of the decisions concerning them? If people believe you sincerely want their ideas and will consider them, they will be more receptive to change.

But if they think you and your boss have already made up your minds, and what you say is only a ploy to make them feel they are participating, they will resent it.

If you sense that Wayne or any other person is going to resist an innovation, take the time to explain why that change is inevitable. Always prepare people for anything new that's coming up. This eliminates the element of surprise, which puts people on their guard and causes apprehension.

Some people resist change because they interpret its introduction as a remedy for their poor performance. They may feel that they have been inadequate and that a change is being made to get more from them. They need assurance that they are not at fault and that any change adopted will be to their advantage.

How Another Supervisor Overcame an Employee's Resistance to Change

Elizabeth T. was considered difficult by many of her fellow workers at the electric appliances company in Buffalo, New York, because she was so much against change of any type. Some of her peers had learned years ago never to even mention the word. But Dorothy R., her supervisor in the electronic component assembly room, understood Elizabeth and knew how to introduce a change to her when it was necessary. Dorothy was aware that people welcome change when it provides personal gain, real or imagined, such as more income, greater responsibility or authority, higher status, or better working conditions. Consequently, whenever Dorothy had to talk to Elizabeth about an alteration, regardless of how minor it might be, she explained how it would benefit Elizabeth in at least one and preferably two ways.

Dorothy's experience in working with other employees who favored the old and accepted ways of doing things was also helpful in dealing with Elizabeth. Elizabeth accepted change more willingly because she liked and respected Dorothy, liked the way the change was introduced, and most of all, appreciated the fact that she heard about the change from Dorothy, not through the grapevine.

Overcoming resistance to change exhibited by the boss

The Problem

Debbie W. has been supervisor of the billing clerks at the gas utility's offices in South Bend, Indiana, for five years. She and the people in her department get along fine, even though many of the billing operations are boring jobs that require the clerks to go through the same routine hour after hour. Although the office is equipped with adding machines and calculators, the clerks still make numerous errors. After a recent city council election, the new administrator discussed operations at the utility's offices with Debbie's boss, Grace M., a woman who has held the office manager's job for 12 years. The administrator pointed out that funds have been allocated for updating the offices, installing a better filing system, and, in general, automating many of the operations. The administrator also said that fewer clerks would be needed with the new facilities—Grace would have to lay off some of her people.

Grace has not been enthusiastic about the upcoming changes in the office. She has put off signing some of the requisitions and approval forms and has said very little to Debbie or the clerks about the changes. Last week when Debbie asked her if she needed some help in arranging for the new system, Grace showed little interest and was concerned only with the work facing the department that day. Why would Grace resist modernization? Is there anything that Debbie can do to help her overcome this block?

The Solution

There are many reasons why Grace could be resisting the change, and Debbie may be able to help her confront and deal with one or more of them. All people who are affected by change experience emotions concerning it; different people have different ways of showing resistance. Even changes that appear to be for the good may result in losses.

Grace may feel she is going to lose something of value: She may have to lay off a friend, relinquish desirable office space, or give up a comfortable way of operating the department. She knows how jobs should be done now, but isn't sure how they will be done in the future. She may wonder whether the people in her department trust her to look out for their welfare. Aren't misunderstandings likely? There are bound to be differences of opinion about what will be expected of employees under the new procedures.

People resist change when they are fearful that they will not be able to develop the skills and leadership that will be required of them under the new arrangement. People are limited in their ability to change— and some are more limited than others. Grace may be very fixed in her thinking. She could find it difficult to cope with a major change, especially if she feels she is expected to adopt it in its entirety quickly.

It may not be easy for Debbie to sense the form and extent of Grace's resistance. She can best learn about it by observing and listening carefully as the changes take place. She can then provide her help where it is most needed. Because Grace has been office manager for 12 years, Debbie should look particularly for Grace's fear that she will soon no longer have as much authority or may soon be replaced.

How Another Supervisor Combatted His Boss's Resistance to Change

When the order came down that management of a paper products firm in Lansing, Michigan, was promoting a reorganization of the company's development department, Robert W., supervisor of the solvents and solutions section, knew that he would be affected and that his boss, Walker W., would be deeply involved. Robert thought he understood his boss quite well, having worked for him seven years, but he also realized that many factors should be considered when a change of this size was to take place. He knew, for example, that his boss would have no trouble with the timing of the change, since the department had been aware of the possibility for more than a month. In fact, Walker had expressed his approval of the idea. But he also knew that Walker resisted change when it hampered the department's regular operations.

Robert decided that he could help his boss most in accepting the reorganization by seeing that moves and changes were made in the proper order and by minimizing disruption while maintaining productivity. Accordingly, he worked out a step-by-step plan for Walker's approval. The plan introduced changes in small doses and gave people time to adjust to one before being hit with another. Robert was aware that adoption of new procedures would be more likely to succeed when the people involved had a chance to move at their own pace. When Walker approved the plan with only a few minor revisions, Robert gained satisfaction from the fact that he had been successful in helping his boss combat resistance to change.

Overcoming resistance to change exhibited by your department

The Problem

Susan B. is the office supervisor of a publishing company in Barrington, Illinois. For about ten years, the company has been actively publishing a group of trade magazines. As advertising revenue has increased in recent years, so has circulation. However, office procedures have not kept pace; they are now inefficient because much of the equipment is outdated and unable to handle the increased volume of advertising and editorial material.

Last week the company's president announced that the firm had been sold and that the new publisher would take over the operations in about a month. The new owner has stated that he will probably retain most of the personnel but that some employees would be relocated and assigned to jobs with new responsibilities. He has also said that he plans to change the format and style of one or two of the publications and to replace many of the machines.

Although the president discussed the proposed changes with all the employees, he could talk only in generalities. Many of the employees are apprehensive about the situation. A few have said that if they were reassigned they would apply elsewhere for new jobs. Is there anything Susan should do to help her department accept the change?

The Solution

Most employees in an organization where personnel turnover may be high can be expected to resist the unfamiliar. Their resistance is almost always due to fear of one type or another. They may be afraid of losing their jobs in the reorganization, of being given more difficult assignments, or of being demoted to a lower position on the staff. They know they'll have to learn how to get along with a new boss or a new way of working. Smoothing the way for such change is seldom easy, yet it's vital to employee morale. When an organizational change affects mainly lower-level positions, it is frequently up to the supervisor to sell it.

Susan should announce each change in position or procedure as soon as she learns of it. That will prevent rumors from spreading as the news leaks out. She should also explain why a change is being made and how it will enable employees to do their work better—it pays to show how a change is an improvement. Susan should make sure that each person knows how the change will affect him or her. If some people must learn new jobs, they should be told that they have been reassigned because of their special skills.

Susan can also help to combat resistance to change by keeping people informed about the dates at which events will take place as well as what will be accomplished at those times. When people involved do not have time to think, their emotions take over, and such emotions are most likely to be negative.

It is easier to get people to accept a change if you are willing to answer any and all questions. You must, of course, also acknowledge the rough spots, the unpleasant part of change. In selling changes, you should try to make them sound simple. Consider preparing a chart showing clear-cut responsibilities. Since major changes are usually not worked out in detail when they are first announced, take advantage of any opportunity to invite employee participation in decision-making. Ask for suggestions. People affected by a change often know the current situation and its problems better than anyone else. Changes work out most favorably when those involved play a part in suggesting ways to implement alterations.

How a Manager Sold His Department on an Innovation

A. Stouffer, manager of engineering services at a large rubber company in Akron, Ohio, took a vanguard position in selling office automation to his people. He knew that if he could get a few of his key people sold, they would be able to help him sell all the others. Consequently, when two men from the computer services section suggested that if the department used cathode-ray tubes (CRTs) instead of hard-copy printouts for some information, the large volume of paperwork could be diminished, Stouffer quickly and enthusiastically agreed. He asked them to make a study of the workload of the department, the content of the files, and the number of people handling records, drawings, and reports.

The next step for Stouffer was to call all his people together to explain what was being considered and what automating would do for the department. Although two fewer people would be needed, Stouffer assured everyone that there were numerous openings in other departments and that he would facilitate their transfer. The meeting ended with everyone smiling and optimistic.

Stouffer continued to sell the change with more help from the computer programmers, who turned out to be excellent teachers. Since they were friendly with people in the department, training on how to use the CRTs went quickly. A few weeks after the automated system had been adopted, most of the cumbersome files were eliminated, two people had transferred to other departments in the company, and the change had been fully accepted by Stouffer's people.

Overcoming resistance to change exhibited by a capable person

The Problem

Helen C. has had quite a bit of experience during the five years she has worked for Acme Products, a building supply firm in Minnesota. After hiring in as an office clerk, she moved to billing accountant, then office receptionist, and now you, her supervisor, have asked her to be the assistant office supervisor. She has performed admirably at each position.

While Helen welcomed the first two moves, feeling that she was getting a better job with each change, she now is not so sure about accepting the new position. For one thing, with each move she had to learn new work habits and new skills. For another, she had to adjust to working with different people. Helen has asked for a few more days' time to consider whether or not to make the move. Why is Helen resisting this change? She was very successful at making similar adjustments before. Should you, as her supervisor, counsel her and encourage her to take the new position?

The Solution

People perceive changes in their jobs differently; some think the change will appear to others that they have not been doing a good job. Others may feel they are being offered positions of less authority or responsibility. One possible reason for Helen's cautiousness about accepting the new job is that she does not feel capable of handling it. Or, she may be apprehensive about working as closely with you as the new job will require. Does she fear you? Do you get along well?

You can help Helen with her problem, but you must acknowledge it is her decision to make. Show her how the new job might benefit her both economically and psychologically. Explain that the job would be challenging, that she would have more responsibility, and that the position would increase her knowledge and understanding of business operations.

When you talk to Helen, watch her manner and her body language to see if you are getting agreement with what you are saying. Feel your way if you sense resistance. Tactfully probe for what she does not agree with. Really listen to her fears or objections and study them. Then investigate to see if you can come up with answers. As a last resort, consider compromises that are agreeable to her.

It's natural to fear change. It takes time for new habits and routines to be formed; some people need more time than others to get accustomed to something new. You, as a supervisor, should proceed slowly when you introduce a change; give a person time to think about what you've said before you bring up the subject again. Most people need time to adjust to a new idea before they completely accept it.

How Another Supervisor Handled an Employee with Great Potential

After only a few days on the job, Walt F., supervisor in the advanced systems department with a manufacturing company in Akron, Ohio, realized that the new programmer joining the organization was a very bright and capable person. Lynn D. had secretarial experience in addition to a college degree in computer technology. Walt could foresee Lynn advancing into a management position with the company within a short time.

But Lynn didn't have the incentive and motivation to work toward a better position with the company. She had been hired "as a programmer," in her words, and had no long-range objective or plan for her future. When she told Walt that she had no desire to tackle any assignments other than writing computer programs, Walt could see that it would be up to him to develop her potential to the point where she would be a valuable asset to the company. With this in mind, he planned and put into effect a comprehensive training program for Lynn, which included indoctrination and instruction on the company's computers followed by a series of temporary assignments in various departments of the company. Within a few years Lynn had moved up to a position of great responsibility in the advanced systems department, mainly because of the foresight and efforts of her first supervisor.

Supervisors can and should be instrumental in seeing that a talented and capable employee is encouraged to seek positions of greater responsibility in the company. One way you can do this is to train the person to handle your job, a step that also paves the way for your eventual promotion.

19

Complying with Government Regulations

Is your office or plant now complying with all the current government regulations? Your company probably is if it is large and has created special departments to assure that such matters are handled. But small organizations must depend on their managerial group, including supervisors, to see that government regulations are complied with. If you are in such a situation, keeping up with the laws and regulations that apply to your operation may be one of your responsibilities.

Because there are so many government regulatory agencies, it is very likely that one or more touch on your specific operation. Try to keep up to date about legislation. You don't want your organization to find itself in the headlines for violating environmental, waste disposal, safety and health, affirmative action, or any other regulations.

Although the problems I have described in the following pages may be pertinent only to a particular organization, you should be able to see a situation that applies to your organization. The solutions should help you to anticipate and deal with problems of compliance.

Complying with government regulations when an employee refuses to obey them

The Problem

Terry S. is an operator of the forging machines in the steel products plant in Canton, Ohio, where you are a supervisor. He is a hard-driving, free-wheeling type of person who scoffs at many of the safety and health rules and regulations that the company enforces. Several years ago the company made an extensive survey to determine noise levels at the work areas. As a result, management installed noise-reducing enclosures around the high-noise-level machines. The survey showed that for some operations the noise level could not be reduced by the enclosures or by any other engineering means. The only alternative in such cases is for workers to wear protective devices when they are in those areas. The forging machine area falls in that category.

Since the noise level of Terry's work area is above government regulation limits, you, his supervisor, have given him ear muffs or ear plugs, as he chooses, to wear when he is working. You also told him that he is required by law to wear an ear-protection device. But, when you passed by his machine yesterday, he was not wearing either device. He explained that he didn't like to use them because they gave him a "closed-in" feeling. You said that he would become used to them with time and you also made it clear that they would prevent him from losing his hearing. You reminded him that their use is mandatory. Today, Terry is again operating his machine without a protective device. What should you do?

The Solution

The primary requirements for a successful hearing conservation program are education, motivation, comfortable and effective hearing protection devices, management support, and enforcement. Education and motivation modify employees' behavior; good equipment enhances compliance. Support of a program by all levels of management is crucial, since it sets the tone for the entire effort. Hearing conservation should be looked upon as an integral part of the company's overall safety program, and rules covering it should be strictly enforced.

You must insist that Terry wear either plugs or muffs when he works in or passes through areas of high-level noise. Enforcement must be firm and consistent. You may have to apply discipline for failure to comply, but several other steps should be taken first. Make sure you set a good example by always wearing your hearing-protection devices. In fact, all personnel entering posted areas should wear them, be they employees, managers, or visitors.

Talk to Terry about the importance of saving his hearing, even though he's probably already heard this. Explain how the ear is damaged by noise. Demonstrate how to use ear plugs and muffs if he seems to be uninformed. Show how noise directly affects him off the job.

If Terry refuses to obey the company's rules concerning noise, you should inform him that he will be disciplined. An appropriate procedure for failure to wear hearing protection devices consists of spoken warning, written warning, short suspension, long suspension, and termination. Although the latter steps are necessarily negative, the verbal warning can and should be handled in a positive manner.

Government agencies hold company managers and supervisors responsible for the enforcement of safety and health regulations. Authorities will not accept the excuse that a supervisor *told* an employee that he must, for example, wear a safety belt when working at great heights—the supervisor must *insist* that the safety device be worn and the employee not be permitted to work without it.

How Another Supervisor Handled the Problem of Compliance

Mark M., supervisor of the power house of a paper mill in northern Wisconsin, made a commendable effort to sell the value of using hearing protection devices to company employees. He believed that good public relations and company support were essential, so he convinced management to offer free audiometric testing to the immediate families of employees. Discovering hearing impairment in an employee's child would strongly emphasize the importance of preserving one's hearing. Mark also persuaded management to distribute redemption stamps to those plant people who correctly and faithfully wore their hearing protection devices for a month.

The company gave credit to Mark also for a suggested method of clearly relating an employee's hearing loss to his or her own personal noise exposure by publishing the method in the company newsletter. All employees were urged to set the volume of their car radio to a *just audible* level upon arriving at work. They should then turn off the ignition but not touch the radio volume. When returning to their cars for the trip home, they should carefully listen to see if they can still hear the radio. If they cannot, they know that their ears have been fatigued by the noise on the job.

Complying with government regulations when you are assigned responsibility for them

The Problem

In 1974, the federal Environmental Protection Agency (EPA) announced regulations about spills of hazardous materials. According to the regulations, which were published in the *Federal Register,* every organization or company that could conceivably experience a spill of oil or hazardous chemicals must prepare and implement a Spill Prevention Control and Countermeasure (SPCC) plan. When the Atlas Chemical Co. decided to construct a companion plant in Zanesville, Ohio, management knew that the plant design and facilities would have to comply with this regulation.

Although any person or group could prepare the plan, it must be certified by a professional engineer. Dean W., a professional engineer and the supervisor of the building and services department of the parent plant, was a logical choice to be given the assignment, especially since he was familiar with the tanks, piping, sewers, and waste disposal systems. How should Dean go about preparing the spill plan? What should the plan consist of and what steps are involved?

The Solution

Although Dean may prepare and certify the plan, other departments of the company should participate by contributing information on operating procedures, equipment, and facility design. All the plant's process operations must be carefully studied to determine what controls are needed and what responsibilities should be assigned. Operating mishaps of the past should be investigated to assure that corrective measures have been taken to prevent recurrences. Becoming aware of vulnerability to spills is the first step toward preventing them.

Dean should obtain the latest regulations covering the SPCC. In addition to the *Federal Register,* there are numerous federal newsletters and management reports that he can refer to. Such publications keep business and industry up to date on the changes in federal regulations. The EPA will help a company with its plan if its assistance is requested. Local agencies have specific recommendations for plants and processes on design of tanks, heating systems, liquid-level controls, piping and valving, and drains and containment facilities, among other things.

The responsibilities of plant personnel in the prevention and control of spills must be covered in a company's SPCC plan. Operating procedures and specifications should call for tank levels, temperatures, and pressures to be periodically monitored and recorded, and for the contents of piping and vessels to be reported. The inspection of tanks and piping must be assigned to specific individuals, and they must keep records. A plant's SPCC plan should also describe the duties of individuals in the event of a spill. Instructions and directions on what to do, who should do it, and how to handle communications help to avoid confusion, minimize the hazard, and hold down costs.

A company's SPCC plan can be effective and accomplish its purpose only if it has the support and participation of management. Management needs to be involved to train personnel, keep records, and follow up to see that responsibilities are being carried out. Moreover, these functions must be performed on a continuing basis. Supervisors play key roles in these activities.

How Another Supervisor Assumed Responsibility for Compliance

Gordon M., supervisor in a steel manufacturing plant in Cleveland, Ohio, was given the responsibility of implementing some new government regulations and standards for environmental control in the industry. These standards and compliance instructions were sent to Gordon from the company's legal department. Although he understood the regulations and knew how his company intended to abide by them, he also knew that he could not simply pass the regulations on to the operating people as he had received them. The technical language of the regulations as well as the lack of detail on how to carry them out indicated that they would not be adequately or satisfactorily met. Gordon therefore wisely requested that the technical department incorporate the regulations in its "Plant Operating Specifications," which contained procedures written in a form readily understandable by operations employees.

If you are a supervisor who has to contend with interpreting and training people on government regulations, you may face a problem. The legal terms and jargon used in the *Federal Register* and other government publications are often difficult for the layman to understand. Don't hesitate to ask for help. You should be sure that your company does a complete job of compliance.

Complying with government regulations when an employee claims discrimination

The Problem

Henderson S., a technician who is black, was hired by your department a year ago when affirmative action programs of area employers were being publicized in the local newspapers. No other blacks were employed by your company at the time. His work for you has been acceptable, but not outstanding. Although he has learned the job, he lacks experience as well as motivation, so you were surprised when he approached you this morning wanting to know why he hasn't been promoted to a better job. He told you it was obvious to him that he was hired only because the company was obligated to do so—that no black was ever going to get a job of importance in the company. Since you were scheduled for a meeting with your boss a few minutes after Henderson blurted out his accusation, you told him that you would get back to him after the meeting to discuss the situation and his future. Is his complaint justified? What should you say to him?

The Solution

If you are not aware of your company's policy and viewpoint regarding the hiring and the advancement of minorities, you need to immediately get the information from your superior so that you can intelligently discuss matters with Henderson. When talking with him, tell him that he is mistaken about his chances of moving into a job of importance with the company. Assure him that he has the same opportunity to advance as anyone, but that he doesn't have any greater opportunity because he happens to be black.

As for promoting Henderson, you should explain that management would promote any person who was qualified, regardless of religion, color, or sex, and that the only criterion is capability. If there is a job opening in the future, he would be considered for it along with other qualified technicians.

The most common type of discrimination complaint made today concerns differential treatment by a supervisor. Even though minorities are aware that an Equal Employment Opportunity Commission (EEOC) exists, most people don't know or understand the discrimination laws. The key words in the laws are "fairness" and "objectivity," but you must be careful in defining those words. They are being defined in the decisions of cases that have come to court. "Fairness" is being defined as equal treatment for all employees and applicants in similar circumstances. "Objectivity" relates to judgments made on the basis of measurable facts, qualifications, and decisions arising from performance appraisals. If Henderson were to complain to the government agency about management's failure to promote him he would receive little if any consideration because of his mediocre performance and his inexperience.

If you have any question about a government regulation that you want answered, call or write the appropriate agency. Government agencies do want to help business and industry comply with regulations as painlessly and economically as possible.

How Another Supervisor Warded Off a Discrimination Charge

For many years, company policy at the utilities service company in Davenport, Iowa, required applicants for various jobs to take general intelligence tests. Management felt that the tests were as fair a method of screening applicants as could be devised, particularly since the same test was given to everyone regardless of their nationality, religion, race, or sex. When an expansion of the company's facilities brought about the need for two technicians to conduct control tests, Robert H., supervisor of control operations, first posted a notice about the two positions on the company bulletin board. He then discussed the matter with the company's personnel manager.

Robert knew that several minority employees were interested in the new jobs and he anticipated charges of discrimination if those applicants did poorly on the intelligence tests. The personnel manager shared Robert's concern, and the two of them prepared new tests for the applicants, tests that determined only the ability to handle the job that was posted. There were no complaints of discrimination later, when only one of the positions was filled by a minority person.

The Equal Employment Opportunity Commission is particularly concerned about companies that give tests that don't have a direct bearing on the job involved and don't measure specific skills. Many companies today still give tests that are obsolete and violate present-day regulations. Knowledgeable supervisors can possibly save their companies considerable grief by discussing this problem with the personnel manager the next time they request that a person be hired or one of the company's employees be transferred.

Complying with government regulations when an employee threatens to sue

The Problem

A steel mill in Bethlehem, Pennsylvania, decided to make a major effort to improve working conditions and enforce safety regulations when statistics revealed that the mill had a poor safety record compared with other companies in the industry. Violations of good safety practice in the mill were apparent also when the Occupational Safety and Health Act (OSHA) was enacted. Immediately afterward, the company took further steps to comply with those regulations, including the issuance of safety rules covering the various operations performed in the mill.

"Butch" C., a roller operator at the mill, is not satisfied with the company's safety efforts. As a member of the mill safety committee, he has continually complained about unsafe conditions and inadequate safety controls. Matters came to a head when a safety control he was testing failed to operate. The company rule required that all safety devices be tested at least once a month, as called for by OSHA. The test tag indicated that the device had not been tested for more than three months. He now threatens to sue you, his supervisor, and the company because of failure to comply with OSHA regulations. What are his chances for collecting damages? Is there anything the mill can do to determine whether its safety rules are adequate and cover the plant's operations?

The Solution

Employees today are complaining more and louder about safety and health problems, and industry is starting to listen and do something about it. About 20 percent of all OSHA inspections result from employee complaints. In many cases an employee did not get satisfaction from his or her supervisor—so he or she went directly to OSHA.

Butch is not likely to take the company to court once he hires a lawyer to represent him or investigates the situation thoroughly by himself. Federal courts have dismissed several similar suits. OSHA does not authorize civil suits by employees who are injured or who suffer near injury because of violation of the safety law. If Butch were injured, he might be able to collect worker's compensation, but that is all. However, his action might result in a mill inspection by an officer of OSHA. The agency can impose fines and penalties upon companies that fail to comply with its regulations.

If management has doubts about the adequacy of its safety rules, several criteria should be considered. The rules must be designed to prevent safety violations, and they must be communicated to the employees. There must be ways to discover whether safety violations occur, and there must be a procedure for enforcement of the rules if violations are discovered.

Read the index of the *Federal Register* to find the areas that apply to your plant, and note the various standards that have been set for those areas. As you become familiar with the standards, you will readily see what areas and facilities in your plant need attention to be in compliance. Your local equipment distributors and engineering design firms can help you with questions you might have on controls, ratings, and capacities. They can be particularly helpful in the electrical field, and since electrical functions are a major consideration with OSHA, you'll probably need to devote much of your effort in that direction.

Materials-handling trade magazines are a good source of information on what you should be doing about hoists, conveyers, in-plant trucks, warehousing, and shipping. Various chemicals publications provide data on the handling of hazardous materials. Some of the engineering and plant operations journals now devote part of their issues to OSHA, its standards, and the problems of compliance. The National Safety Council and the various standards and insurance organizations can and will provide you with much information on OSHA standards.

A business can contest a citation by a government agency if it feels that the citation was unreasonable or the situation unpreventable because of employee misconduct. But a review commission must be given reliable evidence in order for a judgment to be alleviated or dismissed. As OSHA regulations have become more numerous, certain patterns of acceptable and successful defenses have emerged.

How Another Supervisor Warded Off Employee Complaints to OSHA

Rich B., safety supervisor at a plastics fabricating plant in Columbia, South Carolina, realized that he shared the responsibility with other management people that the company comply with OSHA regulations. Accordingly, he made sure that his department did all it could to implement a safety program that would satisfy OSHA as well as company employees concerned about safety.

The program that Rich set up called for a wide range of procedures to be adopted, equipment and facilities to be installed, and training and instruction to be given. After the program had been implemented, he followed up to confirm that all of these matters were handled and that safe working conditions were provided for all employees. Recordkeeping is an important part of complying with OSHA, and Rich personally took on that responsibility. Keeping accurate records is desirable for reasons other than simply complying with OSHA. Written records keep alive interest and motivation about plant safety and health programs, maintain concern for the welfare of employees, and contribute to the efficiency of both people and equipment.

20

Coping with Stress

How well supervisors operate under stress is one mark of their maturity. Usually supervisors under stress do not relate well to people. They tend to disregard the feelings and problems of others in their haste to achieve their own goals. Employees resent this and their productivity falls. They, in turn, feel tension and may themselves feel distressed. Supervisors must be able to cope effectively with stress if they are to be successful.

There are many causes for stress. Two of the most potent are experienced by supervisors: making decisions and taking responsibility. A department head assumes responsibility for planning, executing, and making necessary changes. Each of these activities promotes stress. In addition, a supervisor is responsible for getting jobs done within a limited time and constantly faces the stress caused by trying to increase productivity while decreasing the time it takes to produce.

People who seem to cope best with stress tend to be active problem-solvers. Those who show the psychological symptoms of extreme stress tend to blame their situations on other people.

Coping with stress when you make too many mistakes

The Problem

You are the supervisor of the forms design and control department for an insurance company in New Jersey. Your responsibilities include managing the office operations of adding, eliminating, combining, and revising the various forms and documents used by the company in carrying out its business functions. Your department is relatively small, consisting of only a few word processors and clerks, but other departments keep a watchful eye on your operations to be sure the documents are legal, comply with government regulations, and help the company maintain a good public image. Top management is also concerned with the department's efficiency and operating costs.

These matters require you to constantly follow up on what your department issues and to check for conformance, completeness, and accuracy; those procedures at times put you under stress. In the last few months you've been rather tense. You've begun to make mistakes, something you were seldom guilty of in the past. None of the mistakes have been serious, but they bother you because of their number. What can you do to stop making so many mistakes?

The Solution

Everybody makes mistakes—it's a human trait. But some people make more mistakes than others, and some people never seem to learn from their mistakes. What you should do about the mistakes you are making is to find out *why* you make them.

The most common causes of mistakes are inadequate preparation, bad timing, poor attitude, lack of information, haste, and doing too much. Which one or ones are the cause of your problem? Be honest with yourself. A self-improvement program depends on your analysis. It is worth your time to be familiar with these causes because you'll see where you are prone to trouble and how you might avoid a mistake you haven't yet made.

There are other matters to consider in trying to avoid making mistakes. Work specialists and personnel experts say that we will be more efficient and make fewer mistakes if we do only one job at a time. By following such advice the immediate job gets full attention with no distractions. They also advise us to finish one job before starting another. Fewer mistakes result when your mind doesn't have to change back and forth from one job to another.

Overconfidence in your ability can lead to mistakes, in that you may set very high goals for yourself and then extend yourself too far in a desperate attempt to meet them. When you sense that this is the cause of an error, back off a bit to avoid making another one. And if you feel that a job can't be put off, get someone to help you or else delegate it.

How Another Supervisor Reduced the Stress of Mistakes

R. Jones, supervisor of the job shop in a steel fabricating plant in Altoona, Pennsylvania, was responsible for developing and perfecting miscellaneous small-size steel structures. Because most of the department's work involved custom orders with unique design features, there were many opportunities for mistakes to be made. Jones, however, adopted a philosophy about errors that prevented their occurrence from being stressful to him. He realized that he could learn from mistakes and thereby improve his work, so he always proceeded to methodically investigate what happened, why it happened, and what had to be done to correct a mistake.

Jones first assessed the loss resulting from an error and did what he could to alleviate it. He then determined the cause. After he was sure of that, he discussed the problem with others, primarily those in his department who participated in the work or decisions related to it. When this had been done, Jones prepared a new way to do the job, carefully checked his calculations, and went ahead with the work.

Although he always tried to avoid a mistake, he never let the ones he made put him under stress.

Coping with stress when you feel you can't

The Problem

You are one of the supervisors of the engineering department in a soap and detergent manufacturing company in St. Louis, Missouri. Previous to taking this job you worked as a production supervisor for three years on rotating shifts. Since shift work made you tense and irritable, you asked the company for a transfer to a new job. The engineering department gladly accepted you as a supervisor because of your educational experience in chemical engineering and because you demonstrated good leadership abilities on the production job. Most of the engineering supervisors work the day shift only.

But being an engineering supervisor isn't panning out as well as you expected. For one thing, you never seem to be able to get as much done and there is a constant backlog of work facing you. For another, you have yet to learn a lot about the job—it's not as easy as you thought it would be. You feel pressure to know more about mechanics and electricity and to get more experience. The production job ran much more smoothly with fewer problems. With engineering work, one problem follows another: equipment needs repair, there is not enough labor to do the work, and people push you to get jobs done. You have reached the point where you feel you can't take any more pressure. What should you do? Should you look for another job?

The Solution

Industrial supervisors are often under pressure on the job, so you are not alone. Many supervisors, however, learn how to reduce this kind of stress and increase their resistance to it. A supervisor under stress seldom functions at peak efficiency. In many cases a heavy workload is a major reason, but reducing that load won't necessarily solve the problem. Your personality may determine the amount of stress you perceive in the job. A supervisor with a sense of time urgency may perceive a heavier workload than actually exists.

There are several ways to go about reducing stress. Take a look at your physical environment. Poor ventilation, heating, noise, and lighting can aggravate a stressful situation. Are the areas where you work dirty and run-down? Consider your social environment, too. Difficulties in communicating with craftsmen or your boss may be affecting you negatively. The person who feels he or she must understand everything the first time it is explained, and is fearful of asking for more information, has communication problems. If you can determine that any of these matters are making you tense, talk to your boss about what can be done to alleviate the pressure you are feeling.

Planning and organizing your time will probably help. You'll be able to handle jobs in the order of their urgency and work more efficiently. When your efficiency is improved, you'll accomplish more and experience less pressure from outsiders. Approach your other problems as challenges. If you see a problem as a challenge to your expertise, the problem can stimulate you and give you satisfaction in handling it. But if you see a problem as a chore, you may deal with it only with stopgap action instead of really solving it.

You may have trouble deciding that your job is causing stress. You were feeling stress at work before you transferred to the engineering department—you blamed it on the rotating shifts. This should be an indication to you not to think about again changing jobs, but to alter your viewpoint toward work in general.

How Another Supervisor Combatted Tension and Stress

When Edward S., supervisor of the computer programmers in the motor manufacturing division of a multinational company with its central offices in Milwaukee, Wisconsin, began to feel tension on the job, he decided to make some changes in his work habits and lifestyle in order to combat it. He realized that the cause of the tension was management's decision to standardize products, a move that meant a major upheaval in the computer programs relating to stores and materials. But he recognized that he could do nothing to change that. He became aware of the limits of his permissible stress, and consequently reduced the overtime work he was putting in. He also discontinued taking work home with him at the end of the day.

Edward knew that relaxation in small and large amounts is an effective deterrent to excessive tension. On the job he took a breather now and then by standing up, inhaling deeply and deliberately, and letting his breath out slowly. Occasionally he would slump in his seat to relax all his muscles. He made an effort to walk about for a few minutes at least once every two hours. To complete his attack on tension and stress, he injected some change into his life off the job by beginning an exercise program of walking, swimming, and playing tennis. These activities increased his stamina and resistance to stress.

Coping with stress when you have a conflict to resolve

The Problem

Barbara T. and Denise B. are two of the best programmers working for you in the computer center. You are their supervisor and you are employed by a major airlines company that has its headquarters in New York City. The two women were hired about the same time a few years ago when the company expanded its data processing system. From the beginning, both Barbara and Denise have been aggressive and enthusiastic employees, have liked their jobs, and have done good work. Because of the similarity of the department's program needs, many of the assignments you have given them have a close relationship and sometimes they overlap.

In the last few months, you've noticed that they have disagreed now and then on the scope of their work and how some of the programs should be written. Yet neither one approached you to discuss the problem. The disagreements, however, have dampened their compatibility with each other as well as with the other programmers and undoubtedly resulted in stressful situations. As a result, the productivity of the two women is not as good as it was a year ago. This morning when you saw that Barbara and Denise were unable to agree on what a new program should cover, you realized that you had a conflict to resolve. What should you do?

The Solution

When you must handle a conflict between two people, talk to each person separately. Learn the apparent and the not-so-apparent causes of their disagreement. Since you may not be told the real reason, you will have to call upon your knowledge of each person to get at the true situation. Have each person tell you what she thinks she is supposed to do and how she feels the other hinders or stands in her way, causing stressful situations. Pay no attention to criticisms of each other's performance or lack of it in other areas.

If you can't settle the issue by comparing job descriptions or assignments, bring Barbara and Denise together for a discussion. Review with them the objectives of your department and how their individual jobs or assignments fit in. Try to avoid taking sides. Work out a compromise if necessary. Once you reach a decision, let both workers know you expect them to abide by it even if neither is completely satisfied.

Most supervisors now and then are involved in conflicts of one sort or another. They occasionally will have misunderstandings and disagreements with and among their people. They may encounter stubbornness, resentment, or anger; they may even experience intimidation. All these problems require that supervisors be skilled in personal relations if they want to get the most from their people.

We have conflicts because people differ in their thinking and their objectives. While misunderstandings can often be resolved by simply comparing people's views of the issue, differences in objectives are more difficult to resolve. In either case, you can't manage conflicts by suppressing, covering up, or ignoring them. These approaches only make the problem worse. Instead you must expose conflicts to create situations in which people feel they are worthwhile human beings. Then you can go about finding an answer to minimize stressful feelings on the part of everyone.

It pays to manage conflicts as soon as you become aware of them. The longer they are permitted to go on, the greater they will loom in people's eyes, the more stress will be suffered, and the more time will be wasted by everyone. You are responsible for the productivity of your people.

How Another Supervisor Handled the Problem of Conflict

When Alice A., editorial supervisor of a newspaper in a large midwestern city, sensed conflict among her people, she became quite alarmed. But then, after taking into consideration the environment of the department and the tasks her people had to do, she realized that the hostility she saw was just an expression of energy and ambition that needed direction. She concluded that her position as supervisor called for guiding the conflict as productively as possible. In analyzing the situation, Alice felt grateful that she didn't have to generate drive and enthusiasm among staid and stoical people—her staff was far from that. By not trying to resolve apparent conflicts, Alice gained benefits in that hidden problems were uncovered, viewpoints were clarified, and innovation and creativity were heightened.

Not all conflict is bad, even though some stress may develop. Rather than worry about disagreements among your people, encourage them to search for better methods of doing the job. Many constructive developments in business and industry have evolved from conflicting ideas.

Coping with stress when handling a crisis

The Problem

Henry N. is a maintenance supervisor in a chemicals plant in West Virginia that handles combustible and explosive materials in the manufacture of adhesives. The company recognizes the inherent hazards in the raw materials and has designed the equipment and facilities accordingly, using the latest and best technology available. In addition, all personnel have been instructed and trained on the process and the operation of the equipment. As you might expect, safety is strongly promoted throughout the plant, in the shops, and in the offices.

Yet many employees, including Henry, are a bit apprehensive on the job. Instruments and controls in the plant are not infallible, nor are the human operators. Machines and equipment wear out due to corrosion and use. Leaks, spills, gas escapes, pipe failures, fires, and similar incidents occur periodically, creating crises. Not only are employees endangered, but equipment and facilities are as well; if the incidents are not handled promptly and efficiently they could lead to disaster. People in the maintenance department generally feel the most stress because they are looked to for corrective action. Is there anything Henry can do to minimize the number of crises and reduce the stress resulting from them?

The Solution

It is understandable that many employees and supervisors in maintenance departments become pessimistic, believing that "if anything can go wrong, it will." The typical maintenance supervisor faces one crisis after another. He or she must try to prevent as many as possible while also handling those that occur. While emergencies perhaps can never be completely eliminated, their number will be greatly reduced if Henry tries to anticipate what may go wrong each day. He should promote an effective preventive maintenance program for the department and see that the work is faithfully carried out. Time is his biggest help. If he takes problems one at a time, some may never make it to the crisis stage, some he will be ready for, and some will be delayed.

Henry should also develop standard procedures for his people to follow in emergencies. They should treat a bad situation the same way the plant's fire brigade reacts to a fire alarm. Everyone knows what to do and how to do it, and everyone is aware of the others' jobs. Maintenance people must recognize that emergencies will occur. To minimize the stress and damage they cause, emergencies must be prepared for.

The stress of an emergency or crisis causes people to panic and overreact. Few people think clearly or reasonably when they panic. The crisis takes over and time is lost. Supervisors must be careful not to overreact but to show confidence in their people to handle the situation; otherwise there would be confusion. During emergencies, it is very characteristic for employees to be highly motivated. Executives at utilities agree that line and maintenance crews can be depended upon during storms and after disasters. Certainly, an important factor in their unique motivation is the feeling of importance and of being needed that is afforded such employees by a crisis.

Stress can develop on any job. It usually does not occur among people capable of adjusting to changing conditions. Stress problems rarely confront people who are in good mental and physical condition, have a positive attitude, and are prepared for most any contingency.

How Another Supervisor Headed Off a Crisis

Betty L., supervisor of the typists in the central offices of an insurance company in Chicago, got along well with people in her department because she made a point of learning about each person's likes and dislikes, habits, and families. So she was aware that Gloria R., one of the younger workers, had recently separated from her husband. Betty began to watch for changes in Gloria's behavior because she knew that when someone experiences one or more stresses, it's important that positive action be taken as soon as possible to block the negative cycle leading to breakdown.

When Gloria was late one day and absent the next, Betty decided to have a talk with her. Betty realized that Gloria needed someone to hear her out and help her think through her alternatives, but she was wise enough to avoid commiserating with her. Betty challenged illogical and irresponsible thinking on Gloria's part, doing it by asking questions about specific consequences of a proposed action. Betty knew that Gloria enjoyed sketching and painting, so she urged her to spend more time at it.

The young typist, after a talk with Betty, decided to follow up on her supervisor's suggestion and take a few art classes at night. Within a few weeks she more readily accepted her situation and was ready to pursue a new pattern of activities. Her supervisor had successfully headed off a crisis in her life.

Index